Decadent Societies

ROBERT M. ADAMS

NORTH POINT PRESS
San Francisco
1983

in memoriam
Charles and Helen Frankel

Contents

Nous n'avons pas seulement à tirer con-
solation de cette société universelle de
mal et de menasse, mais encores quelque
esperance pour la durée de nostre estat;
d'autant que naturellement rien ne
tombe là où tout tombe. La maladie
universelle est la santé particulière; la
conformité est qualité ennemie à la dissolution.

Montaigne, *Essais*, III, ix, "De la Vanité"

Introduction

"Decadent" as a term of political and social abuse has a generous range of applications and implications. Marxist propaganda would be hard put to get along without the "decadent imperialist societies" of the west, where most of the invidium lies in the first adjective. For a long time the English said, with varying degrees of politeness, that the French were decadent; the French now seem in a position to return the compliment. Conviction that the enemy was "decadent" led Imperial as well as Nazi Germany to press for what became the two world wars. On a humbler level, politicians scratching for votes in the boondocks find it useful to denounce the metropolis as decadent; preachers use the word to sweep library shelves clean of squalid books that their unnaturally inflamed minds cannot endure. Overindulgence in food, sex, spectator sports, or television can be cited as evidence of decadence; it is the terminal state of any vice the moralist feels like denouncing. Difficult art, like that of Eliot, Joyce, Picasso, Stravinsky, or Karlheinz Stockhausen, can be dismissed by those who do not wish to give themselves the trouble of grasping it, with the single, all-purpose adjective, "decadent." Prostitutes, pederasts, rapists, celibates, pornographers, drug addicts, alcoholics—and, in the eyes of the rabid, liberals, humanists, and advocates of fluoridated water—are either decadent themselves or agents of decadence. As if to confuse the matter further, any time in the past century, it has been possible to use the term as an honorific. Particularly in England and France, artists and writers with an urge to *épater le bourgeois* have taken the term proudly to themselves—and their work, far from being feeble or rotten, has been among the most vital and enduring influences of our time. No doubt as a result of this cumulative confusion, the word "decadence" has recently undergone a stiff public scolding, climaxed by a proposal of permanent exile from the thinking man's vocabulary.*

But though its offences are many and grievous, the word "decadence" is perhaps not beyond rehabilitation. Reduced to its Latin roots, the word signifies a falling off or away. Without an original level or standard of comparison from which the decadent person, institution, or society has declined, the word is nothing more than an incomplete comparison, of the sort dear to soap sellers, who tell us that their product yields 30 percent more suds. (Than what? Sawdust or salad oil?) In the early eighteenth century, when the word was gaining acceptance (Montesquieu's *Grandeur et décadence des Romains*, 1734, was an important early title), people retained habits of thought that made clear the direction of the comparison implied by "decadence." Family trees were drawn up in close detail because important matters depended on them, such as the man your daughter could marry, the job your son could accept, your own liability to the tax laws. Thinking of a family as maintaining a continuous existence over time, one can hardly help distinguishing the good stages of energy and prosperity from the bad ones of poverty and decay—to which, without

*Richard Gilman, *Decadence* (New York: Farrar, Straus & Giroux, 1975, 1979).

undue strain, the adjective "decadent" may get attached. The contrast is set up most clearly in fiction, where "decadent" figures like Duc Jean Des Esseintes (of Huysmans' *A Rebours*), Roderick Usher (of Poe's short story), and the Compson family depicted in Faulkner's *The Sound and the Fury* are all shown by their creators to be decadent in relation to some sort of heroic and energetic past. Before ever we encounter des Esseintes, we are led through a portrait gallery of his ancestors—grim knights, with broad shoulders and martial moustaches, with whom the latest scion is to be both compared and contrasted. Roderick Usher is also presented as the neurasthenic offshoot of a very ancient, erudite, and once-wealthy family; everything about his Gothic castle, his domestic retainers, his arcane library, and his archaic musical tastes is redolent of antiquity and decay—decay from some previous state of authority and power. As for the modern Compsons, they too are contrasted with the romantic originators of the house: a veteran of the last defiant stand of the Stuarts at Culloden, a gallant if unfortunate conspirator, a tough frontiersman, a governor, a general. Such were the men who established and for a while maintained the Compson Domain in the middle of Yoknapatawpha County, and who effectively contrast with their despairing, debilitated, or insane descendants of the "present" generation. They built houses, estates, structures of power; current Compsons are shown to be selling off the land, allowing the house to disintegrate, and either doing nothing or working for the descendants of men whose forefathers were once socially far beneath Compson quality.

In none of the three examples cited does any exterior misfortune contribute to the decline of the family; the families "go down in the world" because of some inner weakness, an indefinable or at least undefined blight. If they were of a different fiber—coarser or more practical, whatever one wants to call it—the modern representatives might still take prudential, sequential steps to "restore the family fortunes." Caught in some net of psychic impotence (a crucial symptom is their ferocious antipathy to time), they follow their own fixations to inevitable doom. By comparison with their forebears, they are decadent: at least in that sense, the word's meaning is not doubtful. Admittedly, the standards by which anyone is judged to be decadent (and "decadence" is nothing if not a judgmental word) are themselves arbitrary. That is why, in the books cited, the ancestors are always marginal figures whose virtues are alluded to, taken for granted in the comparison, but never exemplified at length. They may even be gently derided. But they serve to define the decadence of the descendants in one respect only, the vitality of the family. And the effect one recognizes in literature is perfectly familiar in real life. When a family flourishes for a while, enjoying prestige, authority, and (in the loosest of formulas) success, then dwindles to a series of weak, ineffective representatives who squander the heritage they have been given, we are certainly entitled to speak of a degenerate or decadent phase. From the aspect of the persons thus labelled, things no doubt look very different; they may think of themselves as cultivating perfectly legitimate and laudable interests. (The last of the once-warlike Gonzagas collected dwarves as a full-time occupation, and sold off the family portraits to do so.) But from outside and overall the contrast of a declining phase with an ascending phase is not only natural but inevitable.

What is true of families may be equally true of cities and states; after a period of prosperity, without succumbing to any obvious *force majeure*, they may decline into weakness and ineffectuality. No doubt there are specific episodes in the course of any society's decline to which its ultimate collapse can be attributed. Very often these include "contingent events"—a misunderstood command resulting in loss of a crucial battle, an able commander incapacitated by an untimely illness. But accidents happen to all societies at all stages of their history; when they throw off the effects of temporary misfortune, reform their errors, and reassert themselves as boldly as ever, we judge them to be strong. ("Decadence" is thus not a diagnostic but a summary word, akin to "general debility." A man may die of weakened kidneys, a failing heart, hardened arteries, and forty other specifics; still, if he's ninety years old or weighs only seventy-five pounds, "senility" or "debility" will do as a capsule cause. So "decadence" may be used as shorthand for the condition of a society incapable of transcending difficulties that, years before, it would have shrugged off as routine.) When the Romans were defeated so terribly by Hannibal in the early stages of the Second Punic War, they had every reason to crumble and despair, but they recruited new armies, trained them, stood to their defences, and fought out of their troubles. The later empire, which depended wholly on German mercenaries, which could muster only minuscule forces for its own defence and none of its own citizens, can be called weak; or by contrast with the Republic and the early empire, it can be described as inferior—that is, decadent. When men of the Middle Ages and the Renaissance looked upon the squalid and desolate village of Rome and reflected that this town had once ruled the civilized world, dazzling vast populations with the splendor of its culture, the power of its armies, and the opulence of its display, they could hardly avoid making that comparison which is implicit in the word "decadent."

The Romans themselves, in their later stages, felt the same; historians and moralists without number have belabored the point ever since. The huge painting of Thomas Couture, reproduced on the cover of this book, balances nicely between fascination and disapproval in representing

"Les Romains de la décadence." Towering over the orgiastic roisterers and glaring down on them with distinct expressions of distaste are the august statues of the mighty dead. Presumably the two disapproving fellows on the right are philosophers. The painting dates from 1847, the last year of Louis Philippe. It has been described, rather sniffily, as "a nineteenth-century orgy picture of a recognizable type." Actually, the painting makes its effects more through linear disorder and crowding together of figures than through anything particularly licentious in the subject matter. More likely than not, Victor Hugo was inspired by Couture's painting in his "Décadence des Romains," section VIII of *La Légende des siècles*; evidently decadence has its attractions as a subject matter, it is not simply an inescapable social and spiritual condition.

Artists like to portray decadence, authors like to write about it, and people derive a half-guilty pleasure from thinking about it because as a subject it is *strong*. The person who chooses decadence as a topic is not necessarily contaminated by it, is not to be supposed decadent himself. Decadent themes may perhaps be identified, but a decadent style is much more difficult to define; one need only think of trying to assemble a definition from the poetry of Wilde and Mallarmé, the painting of Moreau and Klimt, the prose of Petronius, Proust, and Gabriele D'Annunzio. Decadence by no means implies mere bad taste; the last stages of an artistic style are often the most elegant, and civilizations on the rise often commit artistic atrocities. In the history of building we may identify periods of extreme decadence, when men tear down palaces and temples erected by their ancestors in order to make from the plundered materials hovels and lean-tos. That has happened all too often in history. Though the reason for it may simply be greed or fanaticism (which, even if brutal and disagreeable, can be a form of strength), it may also be sheer incapacity to see or appreciate the larger structure. And that sort of esthetic atrophy may entitle us to strain the word "decadence" a bit, as when we want to contrast the Romans who freely and strenuously built the city with those who out of laziness and indifference tore it to bits. The act of vision is, after all, more than a matter of raising the eyelids; one has to compose one's image of a building or a city, and that compositional ability may be lost. In the analogous case of literature, Eric Auerbach has shown in his classic study *Mimesis* that the wide and ordered vision of the classic period gave way during the late Latin period to the narrower, more confused, but more intense vision of Ammianus Marcellinus and Gregory of Tours. Gregory cannot even recount clearly the episodes of a blood feud between two little gangs of rural thugs. He doesn't have a structured view of experience, such as might order and relate things to one another. His details are vivid but he cannot arrange them lucidly as Homer and Tacitus, for example, could. The supreme instance of this integrating and relating power is that stunning phrase in Dante where the poet speaks of Paradise as *quella Roma onde Cristo è Romano* (*Pur.* 32, 102).

Obviously, if one values this constructive and controlling power, a decline from it will seem decadent, and in declining from it one can go pretty far. Publilius Optatian Porfiry, who lived in the fourth century, was famous in his day for verses that formed a square with adages around the edges and along the diagonals, or a syrinx or a trireme, or which could be read backwards without altering either the meter or the sense. His contemporary Ausonius wrote a Cento Nuptialis, consisting of verses and half-verses of Virgil rearranged to produce an epithalamium as indecent as it was ingenious. Comparing these poets of the lower Empire with their predecessors, it is not enough to say they are worse poets; they worked (with great ingenuity, no doubt) to standards so inferior that they were hardly literary at all. We may not care to call Porfiry and Ausonius "decadent poets" because that implies invidious and doubtful judgments about their subject matter, but they are poets of a decadent age, when poetry like theirs, perhaps even worse, was the only poetry being written. And the kind of mind that would decompose the *Aeneid* to make an obscenity is very much the sort of mind that would tear down the temple of Jupiter Capitolinus in order to make of the cut stone a cow barn or a pigpen.

To extreme cases of imaginative debility or atrophy the word "decadence" may apply, though it shouldn't be understood to indicate an irreversible condition. But for smaller fluctuations of the cultural level it is surely inappropriate. Tastes change; it is the only sure thing about them. Major artists often have lesser imitators; the fact of their imitating no more makes them decadent than does the fact of their inferiority. Some writers, some artists, some musicians are naturally better than others; there is no reason to suppose that if art is not making steady "progress" of some sort, it is suffering from a mysterious decline, to be stigmatized as "decadence." Besides, modern culture is unprecedentedly complex. The classical world, by and large, knew only two cultures, that of the barbarians (which was unfairly but generally viewed as worthless) and their own. Artists and writers, as they acknowledged a single, relatively homogeneous body of ancestors, could be judged in relation to them as superior, equal, or inferior. Modern artists enjoy a full panoply of ancestors to choose among. In the process, we note, the whole meaning of the word "tradition" has changed and the word has, so to speak, reversed direction: it used to be a spiritual or stylistic affinity that grew from its point of origin downwards in time; now it is an act of choice by the heir from among crowds of competing ancestors—as if the sons were now, after the event, nominating their own fathers. Thus sophisticated and cosmopolitan painters elect to be influenced by African masks or prehistoric sculptures, novelists seek inspiration in comic books or children's fables, musicians turn to jazz and street noises. It has become a commonplace of the day that "lowbrow" and "highbrow" cultures exist to be mixed up, so that a Campbell's soup can, meticulously painted, may find itself hanging on a wall beside a Titian. Since the concept of "decadence" always implies comparison, it is impossible to know (without elaborate explanation and some arbitrary assumptions) the context within which modern works of art should be judged. (Even if one thought it appropriate, the word "decadent" would be ambiguous, implying perhaps admiration, perhaps contempt.) The analogy with "heresy" is exact; when you have a hundred contradicting, competing churches, the heresy of one is the orthodoxy of another, and no man can be a heretic without making a deliberate effort to seek a society hostile to his opinion or an opinion hostile to his society.

For exactly the same reasons, but in spades, the concept of "decadence" is useless and misleading when applied to personal behavior. Men march to different drummers; society encourages them to do so. Who is to say that one rhythm is noble, another decadent? With whom is the so-called decadent individual being compared? No doubt one can and should compare Brezhnev with Lenin, whose position he aspired to fill; and, Lord knows, the current American president, whoever he happens to be, can only be judged a sad falling-off from the heroic figures of Washington, Jefferson, and Lincoln. But inferiority is not necessarily decadence. An occasional inept president may perfectly well be a contingent event—indeed, if one looks at the general run of presidents, mediocrity is a generous estimate of the average capacity. As for the ordinary person, who doesn't set himself up for particular comparisons, there is absolutely no way of knowing what standard he should be held to, since in a relativistic society people for the most part make their own standards. In the current jargon, people are understood to have accepted the ethos that makes them most "comfortable." As they are the best, and indeed the only, judges of that interesting condition, decadence, like a lot of other old-fashioned concepts, is clearly an absurdity.

But if it is easy to stray into areas where the idea of "decadence" is nonsensical, that is no reason to avoid using it, no reason to shrink from thinking about it—if only to become critically aware of its use by others, in circumstances where it isn't, on the face of things, absurd. These circumstances are social; they are above all historical. Societies do have functions in terms of which they can be judged more or less effectual; they do visibly alter in their ability to attract the allegiance of their own citizens and to withstand the attacks of their enemies. Sometimes, no doubt, they succumb in the full flower of their strength to epidemic disease or overwhelming force, and then we cannot justifiably talk of decadence at all. But sometimes they decay, visibly or secretly, amid gaudy debauchery or sullen despair, weakening in the affections of their own citizens and in the respect of their enemies, until they are overthrown from within, are absorbed without protest into another polity, or quietly cease to exist. History is littered with the records of such downward societies; the story of decadent Rome, decadent France, decadent Babylon, or decadent America is recited in lurid detail by moralists and propagandists. Precisely because it's so useful in the slap-and-smear work of propaganda (having this long record of moralistic outrage behind it), the concept of decadence has not dried up and withered away, as on many scores it should have done. On the contrary, it stalks the world these days like a specter of the ideological Brocken, all the more gaunt and imposing for the gray mists which surround it. Very frequently it is accepted without even a gesture at critical analysis by social scientists (*sic!*), who ought to know better. How much of a bogey is it? How seriously should modern Americans, or for that matter, modern Europeans, take these accusations of decadence, which are loud-speakered around the world whenever some faceless, placeless *apparatchik* pulls the switch?

Since the word draws whatever content it has from history, a first step might be to look briefly at the historical record, to see what some decadent societies were like and (if possible) what forces and failings reduced them to that condition. In dealing with these instructive collapses, we enjoy the wonderful advantage of historical hindsight. Rome fell, the French and Russian Revolutions took place, England lost or yielded up most of her once-enormous empire. Given these massive results, the amateur of decadence is in a position to look for proportionate, proximate causes. This approach gets rid at once of a lot of picturesque mythology, since we cannot seriously suppose that major political structures disintegrate from anyone's indulgence in excessive food, drink, or sex. No, the mechanisms of social disintegration have to be somehow proportionate to the dimensions of the resulting downfall. And here we shall have to distinguish abrupt and abject collapses from declines so gradual and controlled that the gradient of their subsidence mingles indistinguishably with the fact of their long continuance. From such a directed overview, however limited in depth and detail, one might learn what some of the symptoms of decadence have been in the past, and so estimate what analogies can be drawn with our own contemporary society.

Such a study, which ranged across time and space to consider all the societies that ever rose to power and then fell to impotence, could easily become interminable. Fortunately, the interminable volume has already been written, twice over. Oswald Spengler's *Untergang des Abendlandes* (*The Decline of the West*, 1918), though I don't think it is much consulted any more, was a vast intellectual undertaking, very impressive in its erudition, very Germanic in its assured dogmatism. It provoked, if not a direct reply, at least a complementary and even vaster undertaking, in Arnold Toynbee's thirteen-volume *Study of History*, which began appearing in 1933. Both are immense books, not only physically but in their range of reference; through these exhausting but informative historical encyclopedias, one can wander happily for hours on end. But for someone who wants a manageable answer to a limited question (What reason is there to suppose that modern America is a decadent society?), they are not very satisfying, and for precisely contrary reasons. Spengler knows all the answers beforehand, he takes the decadence of the entire Western world for granted, and proves his case by saying we resemble, in this instance or that, the eighteenth and nineteenth dynasties of Egypt, or the last empty, sterile phases of Arabian culture after 1250. Sure as he is of his intuitions, Spengler never hesitates to lay down judgments about contemporary affairs, and most of them, over the past sixty years, have not worn at all well. "Western physics is drawing near to the limit of its possibilities," he wrote in 1918, and he thought Cecil Rhodes likely to be the dominant human type of the twentieth century. We smile, no less at his blindness than at his assurance; still, his learning was great, and his analogies, though often strained, are just as often suggestive.

Toynbee, more cautious and more inductive, applies to the sprawling variety of history a formula somewhat looser than Spengler's hardbound spring-summer-autumn-winter pattern. He sees the rise of a culture or civilization as due to a balance of challenge with opportunity, its decline as due to an imbalance. This is certainly right, but unfortunately it does not tell us very much; in fact, it does not rise much above a truism. Everywhere that life survives on the planet, challenge mingles with opportunity; and since too much of the one automatically means not enough of the other, it is not difficult to conclude that the perfect mixture occurred just where the historic record shows that it did, and nowhere else. This is called being wise after the event. As for the reasons why societies decline, Toynbee thinks they are mostly inherent, not external; but he grants himself a wide latitude in time for inherent faults to take effect—as much as four or five hundred years, in some instances. Inherent reasons for decline may be failure to recognize and adapt to a new situation, as evidenced by self-repetition or mechanical imitation. On the other hand, the reasons may be excessive activity, over-ambition, *hubris*. Now it is not very hard to find in the history of any nation some occasion when it did either too much or too little—especially when one can look across five hundred years of history for the crucial error. So again we are likely to find Toynbee telling us that things happened as they did because that was the way they happened.

The present study focuses, not on ancient or remote civilizations, but on our own, and we constitute by far the more difficult and unfamiliar object of study. "Decadence" implies an outside, long-term perspective; the comparisons implied and required by the concept can be made only from a distant point of view. We are too close to our own society to judge its movement as a whole. Like a group of people closed together in an elevator, we cannot tell if the cabin is going up, going down, or standing still, if it does not change pace or direction.

Decadent Societies

We have been in the closed cabin of modern society all our lives, with few landmarks or guidelines to help us decide which way or how fast we are going. Relative to one another, we may move sometimes up, sometimes down, as if we had mini-steps in the elevator cabin, to be climbed or descended three or four inches at a time, while the elevator whirled up or down as many thousand feet. (Arnold Geulincx made something like this motion the measure of human freedom; men are free, he said, to walk around the deck of a ship about whose destination they know nothing, and over which they cannot exercise the slightest control.*) From no society in the world's history are we more remote than from our own; to get a perspective on ourselves, we have to use distant mirrors, analogies that flash a fleeting comparison across hundreds of miles, thousands of years. The unreliability of historical analogies is proverbial, but some light may be better than none, given the perilous course our society seems doomed to walk.

In the longest of thinkable perspectives, there seems no doubt that our present social order, like everything else of human devising, will decay or disintegrate, and vanish from the face of the earth. In the very shortest of perspectives, the next five minutes as I sit scribbling may see such a hailstorm of nuclear explosions throughout the civilized world as will render the question of anyone's decadence completely trifling. Neither of these prospects has anything to do, in fact, with decadence. If the earth collides with a wandering star or nukes itself into a bed of glowing ashes, none of our personal qualities will be of the slightest interest to anyone. But if there is any lesson to be learned from the decadent societies of the past,

---

*Geulincx, a follower of Descartes, is best known today through his influence on the thought of Samuel Beckett, an influence documented by David Hesla, *The Shape of Chaos* (Minneapolis: University of Minnesota Press, 1971).

and we do not take the trouble to heed it, our epitaph has already been written. Perhaps indeed the only lesson will prove to be that decadence is a Halloween-word, all papier-mâché and water paint; but that discovery could be gain of a sort, too.

Meanwhile, a few striking examples of societies *in extremis* will give us a standard for judging what, on the scale of history, complete and proven decadence—warranted terminal—was like.

The Two Romes

THE FALL OF THE WEST

Decadent societies in the sense indicated above—societies that without suffering a grievous external wound began to languish, struggled vainly for a while against minor enemies, and then succumbed to inner weakness—offer themselves everywhere to our attention. We need not look beyond the well-publicized instances, in fact, to get material for a norm defining decadence and some hints as to its gross causes. The first and most obvious example is that of Rome, the experience of the Western Empire qualified by that of the Eastern. Both are limited by their remoteness in time from applying very directly to modern circumstances, yet just because the mechanics involved are crude, they are simple and may serve to get basic considerations up front. Though less distant, the autocracies of the Bourbon regime in France and the Romanov dynasty in Russia were rigid and narrowly exclusive in ways that make them less than immediately relevant to the circumstances of a high-technology, strongly plutocratic, liberal democracy. The examples of decline, if not fall, that come closest to modern America in time and social circumstances are undoubtedly Great Britain and France of the period *entre deux guerres*. They are also, as it happens, much more difficult to tie in with the concept of decadence. But concentrating on these half-dozen major instances need not inhibit us from looking, as occasion invites, at others.

In the west Rome fell rather abruptly. Gibbon begins his long tale with a survey of the empire in the second century of the Christian era, the age of the Antonines (90–180 A.D.). In the old way of counting, *ab urbe condita*, from the founding of the city, these would be the years 843–933; Rome was nearly a thousand years old. For Gibbon, it is the beginning of another story whose ending lies more than a thousand years in the future—May 29, 1453, when Constantinople fell to the armies of Mahomet the Conqueror. It is a mighty story, and Gibbon starts it with pardonable pomp. Still, discounting the overstatements of an exordium, it is a broadly accurate picture that he paints. Rome in those years occupied the central and most flourishing part of the known world. The empire was at peace, yet well guarded; it was ruled by laws publicly proclaimed, and religious codes widely if not universally accepted. Its inhabitants were, if not universally, at least broadly and by the standards of the time, prosperous. Apart from war, the empire was supreme in technology and culture—in law, philosophy, engineering, architecture, fortification, the plastic arts, history, natural history, literature, music, astronomy, geography—supreme, not just in the sense of outdoing competitors, but rather of monopolizing practically everything that was done along these various lines. Roman geography, Roman astronomy, Roman medicine, and Roman building might be "Roman" only in the sense that the Romans took to themselves and called their own what other people had originated. They did not at all mind the imputation of plagiarism or theft; their great epic, barely 150 years old when Marcus Aurelius died, boasts openly of the fact (*Aeneid*, VI, 847 ff.). There could be no better evidence of their imperial assurance.

Two hundred years later, the picture in the west is very

different. To note only a few crucial dates and episodes: in 410
Alaric and his Goths sacked the city of Rome; Saint Augustine wrote, in 428, *The City of God* to explain Roman impotence; about 440 the Gaulish monk Salvian echoed many of
Augustine's plaints, adding a great deal of fascinating social
detail to the picture, in his *De Gubernatione Dei*. Even as the two
learned men wrote, the Vandals were installing themselves in
North Africa (420–440); apart from the brutal devastation
they visited on previous inhabitants of that region, they were
able from their position in (approximately) modern Tunisia to
raid shipping throughout the Mediterranean, harry seashore
towns all around the ocean, and cut off both Roman empires
from their primary supply of grain in Egypt. Between 440 and
450, Attila the Hun ravaged all Europe without effective interference by Roman armies. And finally in 496, Romulus Augustulus, a comic little echo of once-great names, was con-
temptuously dismissed as ruler of the west, his place to be
taken by the barbarian Odoacer, a tough without any title or
claim to a title, except his sword.*

Barbarians Outside

It is sometimes said or implied that the Roman empire collapsed under an avalanche of barbaric hordes pouring down
from the north and east, crushing the last legions by sheer
weight of numbers. The historians and chroniclers often supply us with large and impressive figures for the barbarian armies—300,000, 500,000 men, and the like. The subject is in-
herently difficult, for the invaders rarely assembled their

*The first decline and fall of the Roman empire, written in Latin by Biondo
Biondi (1392–1463), begins the story in 412 and carries it down to 1441.
The very title, *Historiarum ab Inclinatione Romanorum Decades*, bespeaks a
certain grandeur of historical imagination, unusual for the day.

forces of set purpose and stood still for a census. Roman generals who had been defeated by them naturally exaggerated the numbers with which they had been faced. And most of the barbarian tribes moved as tribes—men, women, children, captives, camp followers, slaves, and recruits from the countryside all higgledy-piggledy together. But whenever we get any sort of close count, the "hordes" are numbered in tens rather than hundreds of thousands—and not very many tens. The Huns, who galloped across the countryside in small, semi-independent detachments, were as hard to enumerate as a swarm of bees, but they were a nomadic tribe from a sparse and barren region of the world; they cannot have been as numerous as they seemed, and the suddenness with which they disintegrated after the death of their leader and shrank into a small province of the outer Balkans would have been impossible had they numbered in the millions.

There is an argument that the Huns, by forcing the Germans into momentary alliances with the remaining Romans, actually (though unintentionally) slowed down the empire's disintegration. The Germans were picking it apart anyway; the Huns forced them to stop for a moment and reassess their own degree of civilization by contrast with *real* barbarians. But the Vandals were nothing but trouble for the empire—both empires, in fact; and about their numbers we have some solid information. When they departed Spain for North Africa, leaving the name of [V]Andalucia as a souvenir of their presence, they had to be packed on ships, and for that purpose numbered. They turned out to be a body of 80,000 souls, of whom 15,000 were fighting men. By no means a vast army, yet they had fought their way through Germany, Belgium, Gaul, and Spain, and on their march across North Africa they would take Hippo, Carthage, and Cirta. With calm deliberation their king Gaiseric sailed over to Rome itself in

455 and spent a couple of leisurely weeks systematically picking up everything of value in the town (he even stripped the gilded roof off the temple of Jupiter Capitolinus and loaded the tiles into his navy). For a hundred years and more the Vandals camped at the jugular vein of two empires. The west was unable to lift a finger against them, the east mounted only a single naval expedition against them in 468. Its positive results were nil; in a negative way, it left the treasury at Constantinople reeling on the verge of bankruptcy for the next thirty years. Yet the enemy was a single tribe of not very numerous barbarians.

The final demolition of the Vandals tells as much about their real strength relative to the empire as their successes. (Their name, by the way, has become a byword for malicious destruction, not because they were unusually destructive, by barbarian standards, but because they were Arians who actively persecuted Athanasians and so got a bad name among the orthodox.) Not until 533 was the Eastern Empire able to mount another campaign against these deadly enemies. By then the Vandals, sated with creature comforts, may have been approaching a state of decadence themselves—without, as the saying goes, any intervening state of civilization. At all events, Belisarius, a general of very limited abilities, at the head of only 17,000 men, was able to defeat and in effect to exterminate them. The women and children were sold into slavery, the men went off to fight for their conquerors in an obscure corner of the remote eastern frontier; as a people, the Vandals ceased to exist. After removing them with only 17,000 men, Belisarius moved to liberate Italy from the Goths with an army of barely 8,000 men. The struggle was longer than that in North Africa, punctuated by many sieges, truces, and intricate negotiations; it was climaxed by an astounding act of duplicity/fidelity on the part of Belisarius (he pretended to be seizing power for himself, which the Goths would have liked; in fact he treacherously remained faithful to Justinian). But the striking circumstance is that empires, or at least the remnants of empires, are now being won and lost by armies numbering fewer than 10,000 men. Looking back, a long ways admittedly, to the Second Punic War, we note that the Romans lost in successive years—at Trasimene, 217 B.C., and Cannae, 216 B.C.—armies of 40,000 and 85,000 men. Yet they promptly raised 200,000 more—not first-line troops, obviously, but 200,000 armed men sprung from the soil of Italy, after losses of 125,000 in two years. It suggests a soil almost infinitely fertile of soldiers. Had that soil, after years of cropping, finally turned barren, so that Italy in the fifth century could no longer defend or assert her own destiny, but must be fought over by a few thousand sullen Isaurians on the one hand and a motley array of gabbling Goths on the other?

Debility

In the literal sense, depopulation, though often invoked to explain Roman feebleness, doesn't seem to be more than a phantom explanation. All population figures before 1801 (and most since) are mere estimates, but none of the estimates point to a catastrophic decline in numbers between the third century B.C. and the fourth A.D. Quite the contrary. The highest figure we hear of for inhabitants of the old Roman empire is Gibbon's estimate of 120 million during the age of Claudius (first century A.D.), but later scholarship seems to have trimmed that figure sharply, and Dr. Bury, in his *History of the Later Roman Empire* (I, 63) sets a maximum "approaching seventy millions" for the age of Constantine (the early fourth century). Between the early fourth century and the middle of the fifth century, no catastrophe is recorded that would have wiped out the able-bodied males of the empire; there were enough men, had the empire been able to mobilize them. During the reign of Marcus Aurelius, to be sure, the empire had been visited with a plague from the east (*pestis Antoniana*, 166 A.D.), which may have swept away many of the society's manpower reserves; on the other hand, it makes little sense to attribute misfortunes of the fifth century to episodes of the second—as if the outcome of Marlborough's eighteenth-century wars against Louis XIV were to be accounted for by the Black Death that swept Europe in the fourteenth century. There is no reason to doubt that the *pestis Antoniana* killed just as many barbarians as it did Romans, and in any event, these epidemics don't maintain their virulence across the centuries.

The emperor Augustus, even earlier, had the notion that Rome was declining in population because too many gay blades and fancy ladies were running around town and not getting married; he passed laws penalizing bachelors and re-warding fruitful marriages. But very likely he was judging the entire Roman empire on the basis of what he could see in and around the imperial court, where Lesbia, Cynthia, and for that matter Messalina no longer resembled Roman matrons of yore in their zeal to produce strapping legionaries. In provincial capitals and throughout the small towns of a peaceful and prosperous empire, zestful males continued to encounter yielding females, with the usual consequences. In every society without aseptic procedures, mortality, especially infant mortality, is likely to be high. The empire never grew at nineteenth-century rates, but every evidence suggests that in the fifth century there were no fewer warm bodies to build or defend Rome than there had been in the second when Gibbon described the imperial power as at its height.

And yet it is clear that the empire was, beyond all comparison, weaker. Why? Reasons are not hard to find; the big ones are few and clear. Everyone agrees that the armies had been diluted by foreigners and mercenaries—tough and combative fellows, but lacking in the incentive and discipline of earlier legionaries. The Roman armies of the republic had consisted of citizen-soldiers, idealized in the type of Cincinnatus, who turned from the plough to the dictatorship and then returned to the plough when the nation had no further need for his soldiering. Citizen-soldiers fought under the eyes of their fellows; when they went into battle, their standing in the community was at stake. As they received no regular wages, their profit on the enterprise of war had to come from conquest. So long as Rome's enemies were relatively close at hand, a farmer-soldier could leave his wife and sons to manage the homestead while he went off for a summer of campaigning with a promise to return home for harvest. But as the empire expanded, and soldiering became a year-round business carried on hundreds and sometimes thousands of miles away from home, the supply of civilian soldiers dried up. The service was harder in every way; fighting constantly in the dank Danubian marshes, while living in huts and garrisons at the bottom of gloomy woods, made grim work. Pay was low, and defensive battles provided little chance of loot. On the other hand, because mortality was high, promotion was always possible, and for a while, recruits could be found at the very base of the social pile, in city slums or among the drifters of the empire. But well before the fifth century this source had shrunk remarkably. One reason may have been that the distribution of free grain at Rome and Constantinople diminished pressure to enlist. But coercive recruitment fared no better than "voluntary." In some provinces landowners were supposed to supply a quota of serfs for the army, but when agricultural labor was in short supply, they chose to pay a fee instead. Sons of soldiers were supposed to enlist automatically and without question, but as the empire expanded, the rule became harder to enforce, and in practical terms it was a dead letter by the fourth century. The one undiminished source of soldiers was foreign mercenaries, mostly Germans of different varieties; though we have no statistics, it is clear that by the fifth century Germans comprised a very high percentage of the army. The higher officers, whose names alone have come down to us, were practically all Germans; given the normal patterns of favoritism and discrimination, it is unlikely that there were many Italians of merit languishing in the ranks.

In fact, Valentinian III, who became emperor in 425, ratified formally what had become common practice, when he decreed that no Roman citizen (and since early in the third century all provincials had automatically been Roman citizens) should be compelled to serve in the army, except when his own city was under attack. Later in the fifth century, under Theodoric the Ostrogoth, Roman citizens were prohibited from serving in the army; that privilege was reserved for Goths. This was of course the exact opposite of policies under the republic, when *only* Roman citizens were admitted to the army. It differed just as strikingly from policy in the empire of the East, where the great aristocratic houses of Constantinople—Comnenus, Phocas, Ducas, Sclerus, Lascaris, Bryennius, Kerkuas, and Palaeologus—maintained across the centuries vital and vigorous military traditions. Severe, laborious, brave, and (above all) intelligent, these were the men who made of Byzantine armies the best fighting forces known to the Middle Ages—and kept them that way for nearly a thousand years. (We pluck the passing irony that Byzantium, which survived a full millennium after the fall of the Western Empire, earned thereby among the unthinking a reputation for "decadence" that still passes current—as if any society that endures a thousand years and then goes down fighting against overwhelming odds weren't thereby demonstrating vitality far beyond the average.) But why, then, with ancestral and contemporary examples in front of them, were the emperors of the west unable to build, against the swarm of enemies closely threatening them, a minimally effective defence?

Emperors

Part of the reason that the west could not build an effective defence lies in the characters of the emperors themselves. Many were weak and others depraved far beyond the norm of weakness and depravity even for autocrats. Those who bought the empire for money, who gained the purple through murder and treachery, or who slaughtered innocent populations for sheer love of murder, brought the office into general contempt, along with themselves. We need not multiply examples or recite the deeds of the monsters, but simply note Gibbon's characterization of Gallienus, "a ready orator, an elegant poet, a skillful gardener, an excellent cook, and most contemptible prince" (X, iv), or remark the inoffensive Honorius, with his lifelong concern for a private flock of chickens. He spent a long and happy life with them* while abandoning the fate of the empire to his Vandal general Stilicho. Such men (to stretch the word well beyond its normal usage) did tremendous harm to the empire's public prestige.

Not all the emperors were scandalous, of course, and in a population of many millions, it is not clear that a single man, even when he holds supreme power, can wield all that much influence. For two distinct periods, the empire was very com-

---

*Procopius tells us that when messengers brought him word that Rome had fallen to Alaric, Honorius was vastly relieved to learn that it was just the imperial city, not his favorite rooster—also named "Rome." *De bello Vandalico*, I, 2.

petently ruled, and the way the tide was setting is shown clearly in the fact that not even these "good" emperors could do much to reverse it. From 98 to 180 A.D. the four Antonine emperors (Trajan, Hadrian, Antoninus Pius, and Marcus Aurelius) provided leadership for Rome, the more impressive because their tenure was not dynastic but appointive. Each emperor selected his successor and adopted him; and though these four successive rulers were not, on average, massive achievers, they were certainly able and careful preservers. Nobody could better have exemplified the concept of imperial duty than Marcus Aurelius, who clearly would rather have done almost anything than spend his life in the Danubian marshes fighting savage tribesmen. Yet that was what, for the last ten years of his life, he did almost uninterruptedly. Again, nearly a century later, a second run of "good" emperors, comprising a mini-dynasty from Illyria, gave the empire a spell of strong leadership from 268 to 305. Claudius II, Aurelian, Probus, and Diocletian were severe and energetic emperors; they built walls, made shrewd alliances, won famous victories, and tried as best they could (as best any men could) to inspirit the recalcitrant Senate and sullen people over whom they had been placed. Their success is marked by the fact that Aurelian and Probus were both murdered by conspiracies of their own soldiers, and Diocletian abdicated, well before his time was out, to cultivate cabbages, meditation, and (it appears) despair by the shores of the Adriatic. The emperors as a class could certainly have been better; the better they were (to put the matter very approximately), the less support they got.

Barbarians Inside

Given the reluctance of the imperial populations to defend themselves, the general enthusiasm of German tribesmen to fight for pay, their ready availability for awkward duty, and, above all, the tempting possibility that some of them could be permanently domesticated along the borders of the empire for use against exterior foes, the temptation to rely on them must have been hard to resist. It was the tendency to rely on them *alone*, so that all power other than theirs dwindled and became vestigial, that was clearly fatal. The two empires tried three ways of handling them, as if to leave history a sense of the various possible options:

1. The Eastern Empire, though it was the first to admit barbarians *en masse* and as complete political organisms, by a combination of design and accident, did least to assimilate them. For their admission at all (as tribal units—individuals and small groups had been recruited into the armies, or allied with them, for centuries), the special circumstances of the late fourth century were responsible. Valens was emperor in 376 when the Goths, under pressure from onrushing Huns, begged and bargained for admission to the empire. It was not granted lightly. The Goths were supposed to come unarmed and to give a great number of their children as hostages for their good behavior. These would be distributed through the cities of Asia Minor. From such precautions, it is clear that Valens must have understood the dangers he was running; but the dangers of excluding the Goths were obvious too. If he kept them out, he would have to stand alone against the Huns, with the extra chance that Goths and Huns would make common cause against him, and with further dangers coming from the unpacified Persian frontiers. The Goths were frantic to gain admission, and with the Danube between them and the Huns, they could have provided effective defences for the empire. Besides, they promised an eternity of good behavior, and they were willing to give hostages. It might have been a wise, but it would certainly have been an inhumane decision, and one by no means devoid of risk, to have left this population to

its fate. On the other hand, before admitting the Gothic nation within his frontiers, Valens would certainly have done well to ask how many of them there were.*

In the event, Valens made the worst of all his options. By trying to disarm tribesmen for whom weapons were the emblems of their natural freedom and manhood, he roused their suspicions; by not carrying out the policy rigorously, he left them dangerous as well as resentful. His corrupt officers, by trying to profiteer on the plight of the Goths, reduced them to desperation. By refusing to admit the Ostrogoths behind the Visigoths, he increased his reputation for cruelty; but when they crossed the river anyhow, surreptitiously and in uncounted throngs, he was proved ineffective as well. Finally, those Gothic children who had been taken as hostages developed into the worst problem of all. As might have been foreseen, they did not remain children indefinitely. The girls matured, became nubile, and were subjected to the abusive intentions of Byzantine males. The boys became young men; they could not be kept from learning that their warrior-fathers were in open conflict with the empire—had, in fact, defeated the emperor Valens at Hadrianople (378) and killed him. From being a security, the hostages had been converted to an instant and present danger; they were rounded up and exterminated—to the natural fury of their surviving kin.

Under the circumstances, it may strain belief that Theodosius, successor of Valens, not only recruited large numbers of Goths into his army but gave many of them high positions in his administration. They remained objects of suspicion, however, and around the year 400 a philosopher from Cyrene,

*Gibbon tells us, on the authority of Ammianus, that census takers were appointed to count the Goths as they came streaming across the Danube, but they were overwhelmed by the multitude and gave up their task in despair.

Synesius, drew up a diatribe against the Germans (*De Regno*), as wolves given free run of the sheepfold. But how were sheep to expel wolves? The emperor Arcadius, heir of Theodosius, depended for his minute-to-minute existence on a German master of the soldiers, Gainas. Roman legionaries in the classic mold, tough and tireless, clad in heavy body armor, wielding the weighty spear (*pilum*) and short sword (*gladius*), no longer existed. Armed as they now were with wicker shields and leather helmets, limited for their offensive weapons to bows and arrows, the foot soldiers of the empire were helpless before heavily armed horsemen (*cataphracts*), who might be Goths, Huns, or Vandals, but were invariably barbarians. The emperors could not do without these barbarians, and they seemed permanently fastened at the throat of society till Leo I, who took the throne in 457, devised a dangerous expedient to get rid of them. It was simply to fight fire with fire. To deal with uncouth and obstreperous Goths, he imported from the district around Mount Taurus in what is now southeast Turkey quantities of even more uncouth and obstreperous Isaurians. Like mastiffs and bulldogs, they fought on instinct; and slowly, inexorably, the Isaurians over a period of years drove out the Goths.

For a while it seemed possible that the cure would prove worse than the disease; Isaurians took over high offices in the state, and one of them, Tarasicodossa, his name mercifully shortened to Zeno, married Ariadne, daughter of emperor Leo, and became emperor in his own right. In 488, by a combination of threats, flattery, promises, and diplomatic doubletalk, he was able to get the Ostrogoths under their king Theodoric to move into Italy, where they supplanted and then murdered that roughneck of doubtful antecedents, Odoacer. (What happened there will constitute the third of our alternative ways by which the empire tried to absorb and use outsiders.) Meanwhile, in Byzantium, we note that the resourceful Ariadne managed to rid herself of Zeno as soon as possible and then to marry Anastasius, making him emperor. He was handsome, Greek, unorthodox, and very determined. By slowly building up the imperial armies, pushing the Isaurians into rebellion, and then grinding them down, he was able to reduce them to tools of his own power. It was a slow, expensive process; Anastasius earned himself an unpleasant reputation as a pinch-penny emperor. But he put down a number of insurrections, survived to the age of eighty, and left the empire in a strong position, financially and militarily—the consequences of which are writ large in the accomplishments of the age of Justinian.

2. This resilience of the Eastern Empire in using but then subduing or expelling its barbarians contrasts with two western experiments in absorbing them which took place about the same time, at the end of the fifth century. The experience of Roman Gaul came closest to real assimilation. For a long time, the Roman empire had been accustomed to support the armies defending imperial frontiers by levying a special and quite heavy tax on the provinces where they were garrisoned. Nothing suggests that these outlying landowners jumped for joy when taxed, under the euphemistic name of *hospitalitas*, for a full third of their annual income. On the other hand, there were reasons for the arrangement. The frontier provinces presumably benefited directly from imperial protection; on occasion, this protection may have been not just presumptive but real. Besides, transport problems made it economical to raise taxes near the area where they would be spent. Some of the taxes would come back to local folk in the form of military payments for goods and services. It is not hard to see disadvantages to the policy as well; but, for better

or worse, it was established. Thus when German tribes, mostly Visigoths, were admitted to Gaul as *foederati* (allies, confederates) and began acting as armies to protect the countryside, they were automatically granted a third of the province's annual yield. A modest adaptation of this established practice gave them, instead of a third of the produce, a third of the land. Sometimes when the new *foederati* were in a particularly strong bargaining position, they took two-thirds of the land and left the old Roman proprietor just one-third.

That was hard on the proprietor, but it was also a strain on the Visigoth to give up a life of nomadic plunder, orgies, and idleness for a laborious existence of planting turnips and cultivating prunes. Still, the fact that the division was made by treaty rather than by naked and brutal conquest was good for everyone concerned. The proprietor lost some land, but he kept his life and his wife, as not everybody in those rough days managed to do. Not without jostling and grumbling, the several parties settled into a multilingual, multiracial community, which, for an empire in full decadence, represented quite an extraordinary social achievement. As it had been doing for centuries, the Roman community continued to become less Roman and less imperial—just a little faster. As they had been doing for some decades, the barbarians got less barbaric; they began living in houses, working in fields, accommodating themselves to the fact of law alongside the fact of tribal fealty. It was rather a jolly little society. Roman Gaul, within which Sidonius Apollinaris remains the best-known figure, took a particular interest in matters cultural. Surviving letters and poems make constant allusions to festive, literary-social gatherings, within which the jocund bishop played a leading role. His letter of humorous congratulation to his friend Syagrius, who had mastered the Burgundian dialect, shows at once how rare that feat was and how slight a threat the barbarians were felt to pose, when knowledge of their tongue was a good-humored joke among friends. It is not beyond thought that the new barbarians, with whom the Roman proprietors of Gaul learned to get along, seemed to them not very different from that buried stratum of illiterate, patois-speaking *coloni* with whom they had been dealing all along. In any event, when the Frankish king Clovis fatally defeated Alaric king of the Visigoths (at Soissons, in 486), the idyll of Romano-Visigothic Gaul came to a quick and permanent end.

    3. The third experiment involving an imperial-barbarian mix was the Italian reign of Theodoric the Ostrogoth—the same whom disagreeable Zeno had pushed and persuaded out of the Eastern Empire. Though he had a little left-handed royal Ostrogothic lineage in his background, Theodoric ruled in Ravenna by right of bloody conquest over the previous usurper, Odoacer; it was a conquest sealed with his own hands by the treacherous murder of the latter. But Theodoric was not simply a brutish killer; he may have been that, but he was something else too. Though quite illiterate (he had a golden stencil to help him trace the word LEGI—*I have read it*—at the foot of documents he had understood and approved), he insisted on following the niceties of constitutional law in defining his position. Zeno, to get him to go, had named him Master of Soldiers and Governor of Italy; he liked those titles, despite the subordination they implied: it never did inconvenience him. He was also king, a somewhat more enigmatic title. For he was more than king of the Ostrogoths, but not king of Italy, that being a title without constitutional meaning. Silence being the ultimate discretion, he agreed to be just king. Civil administration remained entirely in Roman hands; consuls were nominated, senates convened. Military power was completely in the hands of the Ostrogoths, who were, accordingly, absolute masters of Italy any time they

chose to be. But for a long time Theodoric never exercised that power; he wanted his people to learn *civilitas* from the Romans; he wanted to learn it himself. His people settled on the land, observing the same principle of division into thirds as the Visigoths had followed in Gaul, but contenting themselves with one-third rather than two. Civil servants who had learned their jobs under Odoacer remained to serve under Theodoric; the consuls Boethius and Symmachus (both patricians and pagans) put at the disposal of this Arian barbarian all the culture and urbane understanding of the ancient world; with regard to the imperial court at Constantinople, amenities were scrupulously observed; a set of shrewd dynastic marriages cemented relations with other Germanic tribes. And the thirty-three years of Theodoric's reign (493–526) were, by all the standards of civilization, an unbroken age of gold in the troubled history of Italy. The churches and mosaics of Ravenna still bear witness to the splendor of the royal court, the sophistication of the culture. Contemporary chroniclers expressed their amazement at the improvement of agriculture, the expansion of public works, the universal religious toleration, the immense advances in public safety and order that took place under Theodoric. The main blot on his career is the execution of Boethius and Symmachus (524), which he ordered too hastily, suspecting certain intrigues between the Roman Senate and the Eastern emperor, Justin. The charges of sorcery and witchcraft brought against Boethius perhaps expressed the last remnants of superstitious barbarism in the mind of this remarkably civilized barbarian; perhaps also they expressed that sense of resentful inferiority which is so difficult to extinguish in situations like this.

Looking at Theodoric's reign from his point of view, "decadence" is the last word one would want to apply to it; as for the Senate and the Roman people, it's a wholly different picture. Thirty-three years of inglorious ease, passed without the necessity or even the opportunity of bearing arms, were absolutely fatal to them. A generation grew up that was helpless to defend itself from the merest corporal's guard. The successors, the rivals, the enemies of Theodoric would remain after his death; elementary foresight suggested that they might and probably would be far less agreeable than the great king of the Ostrogoths. But the possessors of *civilitas* seem to have been so pleased with themselves for possessing it that they took none of the necessary and disagreeable steps for safeguarding it. The comforts of their arrangement with Theodoric go a long way toward explaining the supineness of the Western Empire *vis à vis* their deadly enemies the Vandals.

I have talked mostly about imperial-barbarian relations, which, crucial as they are, amount to only one element in the decadence and fall of Rome; still, some preliminary conclusions present themselves. Before they can be formulated, though, some of the basic and distinctive conditions of the Roman experience ought—obvious as they are—to be reemphasized. For the barbarians surrounding Rome, the modern world has no even approximate equivalent; they were tribal nomads who gloried in war, practiced nothing else, and expected to live and live well off nothing but loot. Their access to the empire was direct, and the warfare with which they had to be countered was grim, stab-and-smash, hand-to-hand conflict; in such warfare, there is no such thing as technological superiority. Throughout the Roman world, transportation was slow, communications poor, literacy levels low. The universal institution of slavery and the lack of any complex technology had the effect of rendering human life cheap— many human beings were domestic animals, others clumsy and inefficient mechanisms. The art of mass persuasion was in its infancy; force and the threat of force played a larger part, even in "civilized" communities, than they generally do today. Under these circumstances, it is patent that the Western Empire (or what was left of it after the ignominious departure of the Augustulus), when it tried to maintain its privileges but would not train or fight to defend them, was taking the quickest possible path to its own destruction. This indeed is the simplest definition of decadence; it is not failure, misfortune, or weakness, but deliberate neglect of the essentials of self-preservation—incapacity or unwillingness to face a clear and present danger. To a superficial eye, the arrangement with Theodoric may have looked idyllic; it concealed a fatal danger, most obvious in the total denial of arms to Italians. Assimilation was certainly worth a try, and on more reasonable terms might have worked. With time, Norman conquerors were assimilated into the life of England and France, Danes into England and Ireland, and Celts into Gaul as well as vice versa; throughout the long history of Byzantium, that empire was defended, and well, by multiracial armies. But for the "civilized" community to surrender total control of its military defence to an "uncivilized" one was to invite destruction.

The Deeper Disincentives: Law and Taxes

Almost as bad as giving one's defenders unlimited power over oneself is allowing them no stake in the society they are ostensibly defending: that was the fault of Valens in dealing with his overwhelming guests, the Goths. It was a grievous fault, which took years of struggle to correct; strength and generosity had to go hand in hand to correct it, and of the two strength was the more important, since no society can give what it isn't strong enough to own. For though mercenaries and allies lend their strength to shore up a society that needs them, unless they are simple adventurers, they are gambling on its survival. What the German tribesmen mostly wanted was protected rights inside the empire—their allotted third, or two-thirds, as the case might be; in return for that protection, they were prepared to furnish the protection of their swords. This was the bargain the empires (and not they alone) were constantly striking with their able-bodied subjects. In return for military service in one form or another, they offered the protection, now and in future, of their laws. Such being the case, we may be amazed to find how poor a bargain they really offered, how little they really tried to motivate their own citizens toward the defence of the empire. Legal and tax codes particularly seemed almost deliberately designed to prevent the folk of the provinces and the deep countryside from feeling that they had a stake in the society's survival. If this were the case, then the various bargains struck with barbarian defenders might appear mere expedients designed to atone for failure on a deeper level, where the real decadence of Rome made itself felt.

Any allusion to Roman tax policy has to begin with the memorable judgment that there is no Roman emperor who could not have been charged with a deliberate design to ruin his subjects—on the basis simply that every fiscal step he took contributed directly to that end. Taxation in Rome was consistently regressive; the richer a man was, the less he was likely to pay in taxes. The empire maintained a heavy bureaucracy, made heavier by the fact that provincial governors and provincial tax collectors had an ugly way of collecting for themselves, as well as for the central government. Military forces, whether in camp or en route, were quartered on the country folk of the district. The rural poor were liable, whenever the recruiting officer could catch them, to be snapped up for service in the army; they were rounded up in periodic *corvées* to repair the roads. Special taxes were due whenever a new emperor came to the throne, and every five years thereafter; the fisc collected ruthlessly, savagely, with a file of soldiers, a jail cell, and torture as ultimate threats. After a farmer had been taxed out of business—that meant, often enough, that he was taxed out of society as well—his neighbors were made responsible for paying his tax as well as their own.

Under the circumstances, it is not surprising that ancient authorities agree on tax exhaustion as a major social fact of the later empire. Brigands and bandits, when they appear in large numbers on the social scene, are often farmers driven to desperation by taxes and embarking on civil war as an alternative to starvation. Monks and anchorites, as well, are likely to be rural bankrupts, and when soldiers, first sent out to pursue the outlaws, become brigands and bandits themselves, the government is sometimes driven, in desperation, to proclaim a general amnesty, forgiveness of debts and cancellation of taxes, if only the people will go back to their farms and raise a few crops. Late in the third and early in the fourth centuries, we start to hear of the Bagaudae in western Gaul; they were outlaws, freedom fighters, tax resisters, numerous enough to set up liberated districts of their own and print their own currency.* In North Africa there were rebellious tribesmen and those strange roughnecks the *circumcelliones*—part heretics, part outlaws, part populists, but all full-time enemies of the

---

*A century later, they were still there. The eloquent Salvian, writing about 440, cannot find it in his heart to blame them. The jealous and hostile Romans, he says, show less charity even than the barbarians, for at least members of the same tribe love one another. In the Roman system, there are as many tyrants as there are *curiales* (district courts); the barbarians have a single chief. As a result many Romans—"and they are not of obscure birth and have received a liberal education—flee to the enemy lest they die from the pain of public prosecution. They seek among the barbarians the dignity of the Roman, because they cannot bear barbarous indignity among the Romans." *De Gubernatione Dei*, Book 5.

Roman fisc. When the historian Priscus accompanied his friend Maximin to the court of Attila deep in the forests north of the Danube (in 448), he met there a renegade Greek dressed like a Scythian, with whom he carried on an extraordinary dialogue, which may be read at large in the ninth chapter of Bury's *History of the Later Roman Empire*. Like the Bagaudae of the west, this primitivist Greek deplored the perversion of the Roman laws, the oppressions of the rich, the harshness of the struggle for existence under "civilization"; on the other hand, he said, life among the Huns and Scythians was simple, natural, free. The conversation was prolonged, the outcome predictably inconclusive. But the theme, that the benefits of civilization are not worth the cost, remained constant.

Country versus City

Hatred of taxes and the network of law enforcing them melded into the countryman's hatred of the city. Stemming originally from a city government, Rome's rulers as they expanded their power remained consistently sympathetic to cities and a good deal less so to dwellers in the countryside. The social structure of the empire as a whole rested on provincial, municipal aristocracies—compared with which imperial authorities were sometimes able to appear almost benevolent. During the later empire, complaints from the rural poor are frequent; apart from the odd riot, often for trivial causes, we hear little protest from the urban poor. Farming in Roman times was grim work at best (that was why farmers were often sought for soldiers), and many farmers wanted to get out of it; the Romans were not always above forcing them, by laws, by whippings and brandings, to stay on the soil as what they called *coloni* and we would call serfs. They became, thus, chattels, the property of the landowner but equally of the state, which was interested in the tax revenue only they could generate. Under this double yoke, it is remarkable that they organized so few rebellions, but when barbarians began wandering freely across the countryside, looting where it was easy to do so, or squatting on the land where it was easier to do that, no wonder if *coloni* sometimes slipped away to join them. It is quite possible that a good deal of what we have called the decline of the Roman Empire was simply the emergence of these serfs, with their popular culture and their long-buried traditions, from under a heavy blanket of forced Romanization.

When the empire flourished, the cities of Rome were beautiful and impressive achievements; by them the empire was judged, and very fair it seemed. Making new cities continued down to the time of Hadrian;* it was the supreme imperial activity, the final product often bearing proudly the founding emperor's name. *Civilitas* flourished in the cities, their theaters and forums; trade flowed between them, and men grown rich in trade beautified them lavishly. Inevitably, the rise of flourishing cities around the empire strengthened, even as it weakened, the central authority of Rome—strengthened it by providing more revenues, more goods, more manpower for the central authority, weakened it by entering into commercial competition. Though this was not as a rule deadly or even hostile competition, it did result in a diffusion of production, and so of economic strength, throughout the empire. Economic dispersion went only uneasily with the centralization of military power; when the army—of proles, barbarians, unassim-

*Hadrianople, one of the last to be created, was the site of that fatal battle (378) in which Valens perished and the Gothic nation secured unrestricted free entry into the empire which they would have so large a part in destroying.

ilated *Untermenschen*—took command of the emperor, it was in a position to use its power against *possessores* everywhere.

The cities had always been glittering islands of civilization in a sea of dark folk—slaves, serfs, tenants, small freeholders, and a vaguer class of free-floating farm laborers. Big landowners tended to be absentees, living in suburban villas or in the comfortable, civilized cities. There they received the reports of their bailiffs and stewards; from there they dispatched lawyers and petty officials to convey their orders to the laborious ploughmen and herdsmen. The cities were Latin speaking, with perhaps among the upper crust a *soupçon* of Greek. The dark folk of the countryside might perhaps speak or at least understand a bit of Latin, but with one another they communicated in their local, indigenous dialects. They might "belong to" cities, but they lived among themselves, in their own immemorial ways, and worshipped their own indigenous gods, perhaps thinly disguised behind the masks of the Olympians. They were Romans in name but not in allegiance; for them, the discontents of civilization had long outweighed its advantages. So long as the free family life of the barbarians did not present itself for immediate contrast, the underclass of the empire had been less actively embittered, because very few of them could recall or envisage a state where they had not been oppressed. But the first cropping of the power of cities, the first appearance of the merry fraternity of rape and plunder, lifted the lid off the empire. Thus was revealed what had been there all along, the sullen and discontented substructure, the *Urstoff* of conquest. Popular, public education had always been the last and least of the government's concerns; what was done in this respect was done by the cities, and it did not reach far into the hinterland. Only minimal efforts were ever made to communicate with the backwoods people in their own languages or dialects; if any proposals were made to lighten the burden of empire which rested so heavily on their backs, no record has been preserved of them. The very concept of a graduated income tax, bearing harder on those better able to pay, never crossed the Roman mind; no more did the idea of conceding some official outlet for agrarian discontent.* The governors of the state made amazingly few efforts to win the loyalty of those classes on whom they were bound to depend for defence of the common social structure. They did not in fact value human life very highly—marshalling armies of barbarians against barbarians, they often gave the impression that the total number of killed was more important than any momentary victory.

It would be ridiculous to say that Rome became decadent because her rulers did not have twentieth-century liberal-democratic ideas. It is not at all ridiculous to point out that in the Eastern Empire, which long outlasted the Western, its rulers were always careful to recruit a stiffening of their armies from their own people and to grant provinces tax privileges in return for military liability. They kept the units of the army small, so that men served with their friends, and granted the commanders of these small units great freedom of independent decision; the deliberate strategy of the overall commanders was invariably to win campaigns with a minimum of bloodshed. Greeks never shared the Roman passion for gladiation, never measured the size of their victory by a body count. They were not so much humane as economical, but to that limited extent they demonstrated a flexibility of mind that

*An occasional limited experiment in popular representation did crop up, the best known the diocese of the seven provinces in Gaul, about 418. It was to meet annually to discuss and to act on economic and social problems. Though far from a democratic body, it might have developed into a provincial assembly of some importance, had it not been swamped in waves of fifth-century violence.

need not have been beyond the mental grasp of the west. For that and for other reasons to be noted, they were granted an extra thousand years of independent history.

THE DECLINE OF THE EAST

On the 11th of May, 330, the city of Constantinople was inaugurated; on the 29th of May, 1453, it perished under the onslaught of Mahomet the Conqueror. Its longevity, achieved in an age of terrible international turbulence, without benefit of overwhelming military strength, is remarkable. Several circumstances contributed. The capital city was splendidly defensible, especially if one maintained a competent navy, as the Byzantines generally took care to do. Located at the strategic intersection of major east-west and north-south trade routes, it attracted from the beginning a rich ethnic mix of Romans, Greeks, Slavs, Bulgars, Armenians, Thracians, Jews, and Orientals, with intermittent seasonings of Huns, Goths, Arabs, Normans, and Saxons.* Though they made the city vital, interesting, and prosperous, these different ethnic groups were always jealous and often openly hostile to one another; their feuds were a source of weakness, even as their commercial enterprise and worldwide contacts were a source of prosperity. Again, though it was Christian from the day of its es-

---

*Vulgar prejudice made it a point against the Byzantines that they set no great store by racial purity; see, for example, Brooks Adams, *The Law of Civilization and Decay* (1895). What is peculiar about Adams's Byzantine reflections is the inverted Darwinism which enables him to argue that because they were mere dregs and lees, the Byzantines were bound to outperform the "nobler" races (unspecified) and so to survive them. C. H. Pearson, an Oxonian fallen among Australians, seems to have originated this logical quirk in *National Life and Character* (1893); among other things, it appealed to Adams's rabid anti-Semitism.

tablishment, the Eastern Empire never lacked for factions or sectarian disputes; iconoclasts and monophysites were but the best known of the many partisans who quarrelled for centuries, mostly over subtleties of the incarnation. Theological odium produced factions in the state; on the other hand, the state was often powerful enough to make use of the church for its own political and diplomatic ends. Byzantine generals were almost always embroiled with Byzantine bureaucrats; the families of the oligarchy had their own standing feuds. At different periods of its history, the peace of the Eastern Empire was menaced by Goths and Huns, by a variety of Balkan combinations, by Arabs, by Turkmen marauders, by Georgian princes, and by those pious, unscrupulous brigands known as Crusaders—as well as by the Ottoman Turks, who finally brought the empire down. Its thousand-year history had been as replete with hairbreadth escapes and desperate adventures as any serial detailing the perils of Pauline. Yet, like the notable M. de la Palisse, it remained alive until just a few minutes before its death.

In the late fourth and early fifth centuries, for example, there was that narrow squeak, described above, from between the Gothic Scylla and the Isaurian Charybdis; an ill-advised attack on the Vandals in 468 left the treasury tottering. In 1071 at Manzikert the Turks won a victory so complete and so devastating that the empire's doom seemed sealed; perhaps that is why Brooks Adams selects the eleventh century as the nadir of Byzantium's decadence. Yet historical hindsight reassures us that Constantinople was alive and well a hundred and thirty years later, until in 1204 the prowling Fourth Crusaders allied themselves with the duplicitous Venetians and actually captured the imperial city itself, looting it brutally and driving its masters into exile. Surely now, if ever, a mongrel mixture of inferior races might have been expected to slink away to the dunghill of history. Not at all. Moving headquarters to Nicaea and making peace with the Seljuk Turks, they built up the most vigorous and vital—as well as powerful—economy in western Anatolia, from which it was relatively easy for Michael Palaeologus to recapture Constantinople, as the Latin empire disintegrated into squabbling factions.

The military establishment that was the mainspring of this Byzantine resilience has already been touched on; it was the creation of those Byzantine aristocrats, soldiers, sons of soldiers, and fathers of soldiers, who not only fought at the head of their armies, but composed handbooks of strategy and tactics, detailing in advance the exact sort of behavior that could be expected of their various enemies. Generals like Nicephorus Phocas and Leo VI contributed to the working out of a sophisticated art of war, which, especially in its defensive calculations, was hundreds of years ahead of its time. Unlike other commanders of their day, the Byzantines did not like to hurl great blocks of massed soldiery into battle; their armies were divided into a number of small and relatively independent units, providing a flexible network of swiftly maneuverable commands. Increasingly with the years, these troops became private companies, recruited and paid by the commander and socially dependent on him. His presence provided a special incentive for soldiers in battle; attachment to them made him careful of squandering their lives uselessly. From each of their enemies the Byzantines made a point of learning something. Hadrianople taught them the value of heavily armed cavalry; thereafter, they were never without that arm, which ruled the battlefields of Europe until the fatal French defeat at Crécy in 1346. They picked up from the Persians numerous tricks of archery and in imitation of the Saracens supplemented their heavy cavalry with light skirmishers. One of their few independent inventions was the mysterious "Greek fire"; they publicized it shrewdly, used it sparingly, kept it secret, and thereby got the most possible value from it. Their navy, though never technically innovative, was active and efficient up to the empire's last day. For centuries on end, their diplomacy was the most deft and subtle in the world, blending labyrinthine theology with carefully mingled flatteries and jealousies to keep the empire's enemies divided and off balance.

On the other hand, the hard shell of Byzantine military power covered a gradually deteriorating economy and shrinking economic base. After Manzikert, the Byzantines were forced, in return for military protection, to grant the Venetians and Genoese a large and ultimately predominant share of the east-west trade.* It resulted in slow rather than sudden strangulation, but from this time on it is not altogether ridiculous to talk of the empire's decadence. Another source of weakness was the church's enormous holdings of tax-exempt land, coupled with ecclesiastical conservatism and suspicion of the west. At a time when all the empire's energies should have been concentrated against the encroaching Turks, the church not only held out for all its exorbitant privileges but used the advance of the Turkish armies, and the panic that it created among established landowners, to increase its own holdings at bargain-basement prices. Worse, churchmen were quite unable to forget their long and bitter feuds with the Latin powers of the west, and so they did their best to impede imperial requests for cooperation against the advancing Turks. In the last days of the empire, it was ecclesiastics who voiced the slogan, "Better the turban of Mahomet than the

*The Genoese were on the whole loyal, while the Venetians proved treacherous allies; but the basic principle of letting foreigners control what the empire needed for its own security was obviously the consequence of desperation.

tiara of the Pope." Even the work of Gemistus Pletho, greatest of the ecumenical thinkers of the fifteenth century, foundered on the hostility of the church; it was church authorities who destroyed the manuscript of his last and most important book, a plea for religious conciliation, at least among Christians.

Still another cause of Byzantium's slowly deepening weakness was widespread tax exhaustion, similar to and only a little less intense than that of the west. In one part of the world, as the other, by the fifth century men were ready to abandon civilization itself in order to escape the fearful load of taxes; not many did so, but that any did was a sign of deep stress. Yet the imperial government was all but penniless during its last years; the last of the emperors, Constantine XI, Palaeologus, could not afford a formal coronation, could muster only 8,000 troops to defend his imperial city against 200,000 attackers, could not even make the dreaded Greek fire, for lack of naphtha. (Yet he and his little band beat off repeated assaults, held their city for fifty-three days, and died fighting through the streets, with the emperor in the thick of the melee, just as if they were not mongrel curs, but Spartans led by Leonidas.)

The form of their weakness thus contrasts with that of the west; the Byzantines were never afraid, though in the end they were unable, to grasp the weapons of self-defence. They were never supine, though their resources failed them. For this reason, and because a thousand-year decadence is a contradiction in terms, some historians have flatly denied that the concept of "decadence" has any relevance at all to the story of Byzantium. They point out, with justice, that though the society became obsolete and feeble, it never acquiesced in its own destruction. It neither committed suicide nor did it, in the elegant French phrase, "mourir de sa belle mort"; it was violently assaulted from the outside twice—unsuccessfully in 1204, finally and fatally in 1453. By then, its trade routes had broken down, its array of satellite cities had been overrun, the territories it controlled had shrunk till it was the mere ghost of an empire. Worse, it had not sunk deep roots of loyalty in more than a small percentage of its subjects: it had not transcended the limits of an ancient empire controlled by an elite class of conquerors and governors whose only interest was to dominate and exploit. Many Christian craftsmen, tradesmen, and technicians entered easily and perhaps even gladly into the service of the triumphant Turks; others entered the crack corps of the Turkish army, the janissaries. In the absence of an anointed emperor (his head was currently being paraded through the provinces), a churchman named Gennadius even condescended to accept his patriarchate, and the crozier of his office, at the hands of the Grand Turk.

The lesson of the Eastern Empire is certainly not that social structures which have lasted a thousand years develop weaknesses; of course they do, and perhaps more corrosive weaknesses as the structures are stiffer and more resistant to gradual change. That Byzantium did not endure indefinitely is less surprising by far than the fact that it endured for a millennium. But in the end, one society dominated by an inflexible elite caste of warriors, bureaucrats, and priests is likely to founder on much the same rock as another. Neither Roman empire could hold indefinitely the loyalty or the interest of its humbler citizens; neither prized novelty, welcomed diversity, or considered the options of openness. Especially the culture of Byzantium was too rich and subtle not to be narrow; focused as it was on the imperial court and the imperial church, it did not reach very far down into the laboring classes or far out into the provincial countryside. The regime made little appeal to the inner incentives of its citizens—to their powers of invention, their individual insights, their instinct to vary the formulas. In all these respects, it was no more than typical of ancient empires; what was untypical was the long-sustained intelligence and spirit of its patrician warrior caste. They made a tremendous difference in the power of the empire to survive. Very likely a modern democratic society, which depends less heavily on a few authoritative figures, can afford to be more tolerant of the feeble and fatheaded in positions of power; but common prudence suggests there's a limit even here.

Cultural Indices in the Two Empires

During the 1930s and 1940s, it used to be an assiduously repeated Marxist cliché that Western, that is, capitalist, society was in a terminal decline, as evidenced, among other things, by the drying up of its imaginative and artistic wellsprings. For all one can tell, this sort of rigmarole is still being recited by linked transmitters of the agitprop organization, though obviously to much diminished effect. (It's hard to convince anyone of Western cultural inferiority when artists of every sort, especially the distinguished ones, are fleeing the socialist paradise like a pesthouse.) In fact, the relation between cultural and social decadence (assuming, for the moment, that both phenomena are real) is far from simple or uniform; it depends on a number of relative judgments and special circumstances, no one of which bears more weight than any of the others. The two Romes, as they have lent much force to the argument for linkage, also supply good evidence for the contrary view.

In the west, it has been traditional since antiquity to contrast the "golden age" of Virgil, Horace, Ovid, Cicero, Lucretius, Catullus, and Propertius, with the "silver age" of Livy, Lucan, Juvenal, Martial, Seneca, Pliny, Petronius, and perhaps Statius. And after the silver age, what should follow but the age of bronze or even iron, an age of general decay, broken only by isolated masterpieces like the *Pervigilium Veneris*, the *Golden Ass* of Apuleius, the imperial lives of Suetonius, the swan song of Boethius, and (dramatic portent of a new age) the voluble, evangelical figure of Saint Augustine. There can be no question that the recitation of names marks in a general way the outlines of a downward trend. Certain valued qualities in classical Latin, like clarity, economy, elegant balance, and ordered structure, were lost in the shift to a "lower" order of discourse; Professor Auerbach has pointed out how authors like Ammianus Marcellinus and Gregory of Tours can no longer *comprehend* the story they are telling, cannot grasp it as a complex whole. On the other hand, some qualities also were gained in the transition, such as directness, energy, expressive power. It's not uncommon these days for readers who find Cicero an abominable stuffed shirt to think Petronius in every way a more stimulating author. A good deal depends on whether one values correctness more than imaginative vitality, and a great deal depends on the original choice to compare all subsequent literature with the highest range and precise kind of achievement of a few selected authors in the first century A.D. On these terms, all poets since Homer have been decadent, and all sculptors since the days of Phidias and Praxiteles.

It is true that classical Latin exhausted its literary potentialities more rapidly than some other languages; partly this was because literary Latin was a completely artificial tongue, far more closely bound by rules, formulas, and conventions than most. For long, its resources could not be replenished from the popular dialects, and when gradually the language was infiltrated by vulgar idioms, scholarship of the traditional Ciceronian persuasion labelled the innovations signs of decadence. In much the same way genteel Bostonians rejected Whitman as an uncouth barbarian; our contemporary judgment is likely to be that they, rather than he, should be labelled effete and in that sense decadent. As between the two empires, Greek and Latin, the Greek shows a much less clear pattern than the Latin of slow rise, brief achievement, and "inevitable" decline. There is no way to arrange Homer, the dramatists, the historians, the philosophers, the pastoral poets, the romance writers, the moralists like Plutarch, and the Christian Greeks in any simple schema.

Many arts other than the verbal enter into one's estimate of a nation's cultural estate, whether flourishing or feeble, but we are handicapped in dealing with most of them by historical circumstances. All the ancient Greek painting has disappeared, and Rome, both in painting and sculpture, rarely did much more than copy the Greeks—so what decadence amounts to depends on what you choose to compare with what. This is by no means a free choice; accident has already determined most of it. Almost all the finest statues of Byzantium were stolen or destroyed by the Latin conquerors (we have a list of them, nothing more—*vox et praeterea nihil*); the slim remainder fell victim to the Turks of 1453. The artistic history of Byzantium has had to be painfully assembled from fragments of ivory and gold scattered across the face of Europe, from mosaics dug out of mountains of debris or hidden behind plaster and whitewash. What seems definite is that there was no steady progression or decline in the arts that Byzantium practiced most assiduously. Rather, periods of flagging inspiration alternated with periods of renewed vitality and fresh invention. Santa Sophia itself is a creation of the sixth century, though all its original mosaics were destroyed in the eighth century, and the few magnificent panels that came through two terrible sieges are mostly of the eleventh century; it is hard to describe *them* as works of decadence. The ivories, tapestries, chalices, and sculptures of the eleventh century are, as a class, works of singular beauty; they come to us from the period commonly denounced as the corrupt nadir of Byzantine civilization. A literary man of that age, Michael Psellus, is often described as the Voltaire of Byzantine letters; he was extraordinarily versatile in his interests, with a keen style, an insatiable curiosity, and so rich an understanding of Plato that he became a major figure through whom the influence of that philosopher was transmitted to the west. In the late thirteenth century, Cimabue, the first major painter of Italy, took as models for his art the work of Byzantine contemporaries; his great-grandson was in the imperial city, still studying the principles of Byzantine art, when the Turkish conquest changed everyone's plans. The builders of St. Mark's Cathedral in Venice, during the many centuries of its construction and decoration, rarely took their eyes off the Byzantine example; they would scarcely have been so assiduous had they thought the eastern originals either obsolete or inferior.

Because it is vivid and dramatic, the decline of classical culture in the west does seem to foreshadow a decline in the political energies of the society; in both, we sense a loss of constructional power, an incapacity to hold things together. It is not always clear whether the works exemplifying this quality should be called "primitive" or "decadent"; a work like Martianus Capella's early-fifth-century mélange called "The Marriage of Mercury and Philology" is more like an uncouth new voice than an exhausted old one. On the other hand, Gregory of Tours, in the sixth century, does seem to feel that his language is inadequate, that a better "grammaticus" than he is needed to tell his story. He is decadent in knowing what ought to be done and being unable to do it—a true barbarian wouldn't even have known. But the pattern of the Eastern Empire, because it is less dramatic, has been less regarded. The society's origins were late classical, so the standards for decadence were not clear to begin with. Not having as many half-assimilated barbarians as the west, the east did not mix the primitive with the decadent in anything like the same way. The cultural ups and downs of the Eastern Empire do not coincide significantly with its periods of military-political prosperity and depression. Above all, the abruptness and compression of the Western Empire's decline fit it to point a moral and adorn a tale; the thousand-year history of the east admits too many contingent complexities. As the concept of decadence generally includes a large moral component, exemplary consequences are supposed to follow hard on the demonstrated condition. Occasionally they do, but mostly things aren't that simple.

Looking for a moment beyond the two Romes to France and Russia in the last stages of their respective declines toward 1789 and 1917, we find little evidence of cultural decadence to warn of the impending catastrophe. Quite the contrary. The France of Voltaire and Rousseau, of Montesquieu, Diderot, and the *philosophes* was so far from sinking into mental apathy that it was among the most brilliant history has known. To recite the names of the *philosophes* and their no less brilliant mistresses, patronesses, and birds of passage would be gratuitous; they were the best and brightest of their day. Quesnay and Turgot, could they have made themselves heard by a government deaf to reason, could have reformed the economy in a way conceivably to avert, or in any case to minimize, the worst excesses of the revolution. Novels like *Manon Lescaut* and *Dangerous Acquaintances*, the plays of Beaumarchais, the authors of memoirs, critiques, books of travel, fantasies, grotesques, and commentaries too numerous to recite, all testify to the intellectual vigor and versatility of the old regime. It was an era rich in scientific thinkers, in mathematicians, chemists, natural historians (the celebrated Buffon, for example), astronomers, and astronomical mythographers of the ingenuity of Dupuis. In the field of "hard" science, the names of Laplace, Lagrange, and Lavoisier need merely be mentioned; their achievements could hardly have occurred in an age of mental torpor and decay.

The notion that cultural decadence is directly linked to social decadence meets its ultimate refutation in the record of prerevolutionary Russia. If ever a society was tottering toward dissolution, it was Romanov Russia in the first few years of the twentieth century. All but bankrupt, it was shakily propped on a ramshackle structure of French loans; its autocracy was simply out of touch with reality, its military establishment incompetent, its financial machinery in a shambles. A strong and active terrorist-revolutionary movement had sunk deep roots within Russia and enjoyed wide support abroad. Any sensible prognosis of the society's future would have had to be very reserved indeed. Yet in those last nightmare years before the revolution, Russian culture flowered beyond any in Europe, and in regions where Russian culture had never flourished before and has not done since. One need only mention painters like Kandinsky, Soutine, Chagall, sculptors like Lipchitz, Gabo, Archipenko, the extraordinary balletic combination of Bakst, Stravinsky, Diaghilev, and Nijinsky—not to mention men like Blok, Rachmaninov, Kuprin, Prokofiev, Gorky, Mayakovsky, Burliuk—the list need not be eked out with minor names. It was a tremendous imaginative explosion, and it occurred when by every canon of social determinism the culture of Czarist Russia should have been in the last stages of imaginative debility.

There is an ancient simplicity which, instead of correspondence, proposes an inverse relation between culture and social vigor—the more of the one, the less of the other. Some Huns invading Greece were thinking on this track when they decided not to torch the libraries because, while the Greeks were reading books, they would not be making conspiracies against Huns. Though obviously rather limited, Hunnish thinking, this isn't a completely idiot idea; insofar as a society needs a lot of roughnecks to fight off barbarians, it is unlikely to get what it needs by training esthetes and bookworms. On the other hand, loutishness and ignorance *per se* are no guarantees of social health. The sum of the matter is that all generalizations collapse when applied to the second or third instance. Between the vigor or debility of a society and the debility or vigor of its culture all relationships are possible, none is necessary or uniform. Deducing one condition from the other is out of the question. It is a negative conclusion, but positive at least in the sense that it clears the field of a good deal of claptrap, leaving us to concentrate on societies that demonstrated their social decadence by failing to fulfill their essential functions as societies.

France and Russia

In the moral framework of Cecil B. De Mille movies and Marxist propaganda, the decadence that led to collapse of France's Bourbon dynasty in 1789 must be traced to the Deer Park of Louis Quinze and the milkmaid make-believe of Marie Antoinette. Similarly, the disintegration of Russia's Romanov dynasty in 1917 would not be thinkable without lurid tales of Rasputin and his orgies. Let us try to dispense with these hackneyed dramatic props.

LA CANAILLE, LES ARISTOS

The old regime in France, which dissolved even more abruptly than the Roman Empire of the West, had much in common with that earlier instance. It was an autocracy within which priests, warriors, and bureaucrats occupied positions of entrenched privilege. It relied, to an extent it did not appreciate, on the good will, active or passive, of social classes whose loyalty it had done nothing to enlist, whose energies it had done everything to frustrate. Its ruling classes were opulent and amazingly, almost pathologically, obtuse; its legal and tax structures were at once inefficient and oppressive. Nothing equivalent to the barbarian invasions threatened France in the years before her collapse; all the more striking, therefore, are the inner stresses that by themselves sufficed to bring down the regime.

French society was an ancient patchwork of injustices and anomalies—so we find all observers of the *ancien régime* agreeing. The three estates might in feudal times have corresponded with a sort of social reality the clergy, who alone could read and who possessed great estates, the nobles, eminent in war and also possessing great estates—these classes "naturally" took precedence over the common folk, whose only claim to consideration was their numbers. But by the eighteenth century, there were laymen aplenty who could read and reason better than the clerics; as Napoleon would discover, there were men among the sons of bakers and notaries who would make better warriors than descendants of the paladins. Aristocracy had been watered down, across the centuries, by the ennobling of courtiers and placemen; the clergy too had been watered down, not at the level of the parish priest, but by the multiplication of abbés, vicars, almoners, freethinking bishops, and ecclesiastical courtiers—aspiring little Richelieus, many of them, who monopolized the privileges and spoke in the name of the "clergy." On the other side, the "third estate" no longer consisted of illiterate serfs; it now included ambitious lawyers, cosmopolitan traders, a few manufacturers, many businessmen of great energy and ability who found it humiliating to be excluded from the privileges and responsibilities of administration. Crude numbers reveal a crude imbalance of power: the privileged orders, counting aristocracy and clergy together and defining both with the utmost liberality, amounted to a third of a million persons (100,000 clergy, 200,000 aristocrats); the third estate, consisting of everybody else, numbered some twenty-two and

one-half million.* Yet when the States General were convened in 1789, the third estate had to fight tooth and nail to
keep from being outvoted, two to one, by a bare two percent
of the population.

Taxation under the old regime was deliberately ar-
ranged to fall as heavily as possible on those least able to pay
it. The clergy were exempt altogether from taxation of any
sort; all the nobility were exempt from some taxation, and
some were exempt from all. The *taille* was paid only by the
peasantry, who were liable also for road service (*corvées*),
though they had least occasion of anybody to use the roads;
as in ancient Rome, they were also liable for quartering troops
on the move, providing them with vehicles, draft animals, and
food. The tax known as *vingtième* was theoretically levied on

---

*Putting numbers on a description of the old regime is extremely difficult,
but not in the end very important. The aristocrats have been estimated at
half as many and twice as many as the number given here. But there is every
reason not to be strict. Titles of honor exercise wide magnetic attraction;
great houses develop and maintain many collateral lines, sprung from cou-
sins, daughters married into other families, bastards, god-children, and
the like. The aristocratic families of the old regime were much more like
clans than like our modern nuclear families. Thus, some 25,000 aristocratic families, averaging closer to ten than to five components, would
yield a class of about a quarter million. To these must be added the entire
body of the upper clergy who, though counted separately, were blue-
blooded to a man.

Numbers, however, are unimportant, since elites by definition exercise
their influence in other ways. A striking example of that fact is found within
the aristocracy itself. The number of those eighteenth-century aristocrats
who could trace their lineage back to the days of Pepin (not to mention the
very first Frankish monarch, Clovis) was negligible, frivolous. Yet they imposed their mystique on the much larger body of families who owed their
ennoblement to a particularly shrewd civil servant or supple counsellor of
the past century or two.

all lay subjects, but was so widely and easily avoided by the wily (especially since the aristocracy held all the higher administrative offices and actively aspired to monopolize all the lower ones too) that in effect it fell only on the peasantry. *Capitation*, sometimes translated as a poll tax but really a primitive income tax, was paid only by peasants. The salt tax or *gabelle* was irksome enough in itself; doubly irksome in that some districts were completely exempt from it; triply irksome in that, to augment the take (most of which went to tax collectors and tax farmers, rather than the government), districts were required to buy more salt than they needed at prices far higher than were justified. Peasants of course all paid tithe; they also paid local excise taxes on practically all the commodities of life; they paid tolls on goods brought to market, carried along roads, or shipped on rivers; they paid an extra kind of quitrent known in many districts as *champart*. When they owned pigeon coops or rabbit warrens, they paid tax on them; for pigeons kept in the lord's cote and rabbits allowed to run free for his sport he paid no tax, and they could not be killed, no matter how much of the peasant's crop they devoured. The standing grain could be ridden over by aristocrats, who all enjoyed hunting privileges. Mills, bakeries, and wine presses all paid special fees for the privilege of operating, the cost of which was inevitably passed on to the peasantry. Lords of the manor maintained feudal courts through which they distributed "justice" to their tenants and privileges to themselves—monopolies of the good things, exemptions from the bad. (Controlling these courts, they were naturally eager to have the peasantry well represented in provincial assemblies.) Special fees were due whenever leases lapsed or changed hands. For esthetic effect, lords were encouraged to plant trees along the highways; the manor house got the trimmings for firewood, and shade from the trees effectively reduced the growing

space in the peasant's field. So many varieties of personal service and so many special payments were imposed on the peasantry (few of whom could read or understand the statutes)
that they were simply overwhelmed. The inhabitants of Erce-
ville near Orléans listed among their complaints that they
were asked to pay a tax of one percent on the value of the rings
and jewels provided for the bride in a marriage contract. The
tax, they declared, had been imposed only in the past six
months, on what authority they could not know, but it had
been made retroactive to cover all marriage contracts over the
past twenty years. There was an entire vocabulary of taxes to
pry money loose from working people: *aides, contrôles, insin-
uations, centième denier, amortissements, francs-fiefs, avenages,
tasques, lods et ventes, fouages*, etc., etc.

The weight of this taxation falling on the peasantry
would have reduced them to misery had they been the most
scientific cultivators in Europe; it had the particular effect
of making them among the most backward. They could not
afford improvements, they had no reason to make improvements, when every last scrap of surplus would be taken from
them, whatever their output. Depressing the peasant had a
particularly grim effect because in France under the old regime there was remarkably little industrial life. Partly, this
may have been due to the revocation, in 1685, of the Edict of
Nantes; revoking their religious rights drove out of the country many Huguenots, who had been the mainstay of the weav-
ing industry. In addition, a sharp division between aristocracy
and bourgeoisie made it disgraceful for a younger son to enter
commerce, easy and advantageous for him to take a privileged
position in the church or the army. Lavish distribution of hon-
ors and awards by the central monarchy encouraged landowners to leave their estates and cultivate favor at Versailles instead. Arthur Young, visiting France in 1787, found himself

vexed and provoked at every turn by evidence of ill agricultural management and selfish rack-renting by the landlords:

> *The same wretched country continues to La Loge; the fields are*
> *scenes of pitiable management as the houses are of misery. Yet all*
> *this country is highly improvable, if they knew what to do with it; the*
> *property, perhaps, of some of those glittering beings who figured in*
> *the procession the other day at Versailles. Heaven grant me patience*
> *while I see a country thus neglected—and forgive me the oaths I*
> *swear at the absence and ignorance of the possessors.*

Indeed, the worst aspect of French rural society was
hardly accessible to a tourist like Young. Far below the rank
of the possessors and outside even the society of the exploited
peasants with their miserably inadequate tenant farms, buried
deep in the back country for the most part, was an indefinite but large number of landless and homeless poor, ragged
skulkers in the outlying heaths and marshes. In the terminology of the time, they were either vagrants or brigands; nobody
counted them, for obvious reasons, but they were many. An
estimate of 1790 proposed that close to half of the French
population—ten out of twenty-three million—were in need
of relief; and of these, three million were absolute paupers,
who existed only by begging. When the revolution, which was
first made by lawyers and parliamentarians, spread outward
and downward, through the urban poor and into the countryside, it was these "vagrants and brigands" (spiritually akin to
if not descended from the ancient Bagaudae, outlaws and tax
resistors of Roman Gaul) who crept out of the woods to as-
sault, with clubs, pitchforks, and torches, the glittering country houses of the gentry.

The analogy with ancient Rome makes itself felt, not
only in the very large number of these outcasts but in the attitude of the aristocracy toward them and toward the third es-

tate in general—even toward the monarchy. For some of the French aristocrats, those more ancient gentry in particular who distinguished themselves as "of the sword" rather than "of the robe," claimed descent (how accurately we had better not ask) from those Frankish tribesmen who in the time of Clovis had conquered and occupied Romano-Visigothic Gaul. We cannot, and they very much did not want to, say they had conquered *under* Clovis. Germanic tribes and the Franks particularly chose their leaders freely and disdained permanent submission to them—their kingship amounted to being *dux bellorum*, and little else. Consequently the estates seized by the original Franks, which in the eighteenth century were the estates of their lineal descendants, had been won by right of individual conquest: neither Clovis nor any other king had given them or could give them. And toward the villeins or serfs who worked these estates, the conquerors and their descendants owed no obligations or considerations whatever. They were not of the same nation, they were scarcely of the same species.

It goes without saying that this view of the aristocracy as a nation within a nation, independent of monarchy and third estate alike, was not held by all aristocrats, and by those who did subscribe to it was held rather as a myth than as a complete political doctrine. Still it did find overt expression in the eighteenth century, first as an abstract tenet, then in quite concrete political acts. The very year that Louis XVI assumed the throne (1747), Mirabeau's father, in his *Testament politique*, advocated that the baronage resume from the monarchy some of the lapsed or usurped powers that in feudal times they used to exercise on their own authority. The same thought or something like it can be found in Montesquieu, whose *Spirit of the Laws* (1748) has been called a handbook of aristocratic beliefs. Moves to enlarge aristocratic monopoly of all government offices, to assert exclusive aristocratic rights to all senior posts in the army and navy, to secure aristocratic command of provincial assemblies, to place aristocrats in superior offices of the church, all pointed in this direction. Because the aristocracy was an exclusive, ingrown body, its members communicating almost entirely with one another, its idiosyncratic outlook was accentuated, exaggerated. Absentee landlordism became the rule, partly because the gentry found it disagreeable to live among uncouth peasants, partly because pleasure and profit combined to draw them to the court, where they basked in each other's society. Because aristocrats administered the king's own properties, it was easy for a count who had been granted a pension to arrange with his cousin the duke to exchange it for an estate from the king's demesne, then to trade that estate for a better one, and so on. Most notable of all, the aristocracy's sense of its own importance led many of its members (those "of the robe" no less than those "of the sword") to oppose or undermine efforts by the monarchy and its servants to cut expenses and rationalize the tax system. Some courtiers sincerely thought their offices and perquisites belonged to them and their descendants in perpetuity—at the very mention of economies, they grew furiously indignant. Others saw in the financial embarrassments of the central government a chance to enlarge the authority of the provincial assemblies that they were confident of dominating. For them, government deficits were not a misfortune but a blessed advantage. By refusing on various pretexts to vote the financial reforms proposed by the king's ministers, they hoped to force the calling of the States General, which they anticipated being able to control as easily as they controlled the provincial estates.

This strong, but extremely vague, magnetism attaching to the idea of the States General was an important element of instability in the prerevolutionary situation. Everybody, with the possible exception of Louis XVI, yearned for the convoking of this body; hardly anybody could agree on what it would actually do when it was assembled. Reformation of abuses was expected from the States General—but which abuses? Rights would certainly be affirmed—but which rights, and whose? Without lingering over these secondary questions, the vast majority of the nation agreed that the States General must definitely be assembled. Curious it now appears that they should all have been so positive on the necessity of an institution which no man living had experienced. Actually, the States General had accomplished very little in 1614, the last time they were convened; had they remained in control of the privileged classes, they would have accomplished very little in 1789. What made them a revolutionary body was the "doubling of the third," that is, double representation of the third estate, combined with voting by head, rather than by order. (Individual voting enabled the third estate to capture some votes from liberal aristocrats and clergymen; voting by order would have assured that the third estate was always outvoted by two to one.) These two measures, neither fought *à l'outrance* by the privileged orders, sufficed to convert the staid three-part meeting of the States General (for which the aristocrats themselves had clamored) into a revolutionary unicameral National Assembly. Even had they fought it, the privileged classes could probably not have postponed indefinitely the calling of the States General, but that they should have been misled by their own archaic quarrel with the crown into swelling the call for the body that would destroy them was a signal piece of social blindness. It can't be said that the old regime consciously and deliberately brought about its own destruction, but in demanding a meeting of the States General, the ruling classes certainly twisted the rope that would be used to hang them. When the Roman senate took swords out

of the hands of Italians and placed them in the hands of Theodoric's Ostrogoths, it did no more to seal its own fate.

The Alternative

Fundamentally, the pressure on the *ancien régime* that led to
the calling of the States General and so to the National Assembly and so to the Committee of Public Safety and the reign
of terror was economic. Despite the best efforts of Turgot,
Necker, Calonne, and Brienne, the government was effec-
tually bankrupt well before 1789. For years, for decades, the
treasury had spent too much and taken in too little. The ministers regularly recommended remedies for the situation, so
far from revolutionary in their import that most of them de-
rived from ideas proposed in 1698 by Marshal Vauban. Most
reformers drew the commonsense conclusion from an unbal-
anced budget that income must be increased and expenses
cut. François Quesnay in his celebrated *Tableau économique*
(1757–58) proposed to revamp the whole economy by reduc-
ing expenditures on luxury items, foreign imports, and interest payments, while stimulating productive enterprises, particularly agriculture. The basic idea, good enough to be re-
cycled in twentieth-century Britain, was that there were too
few producers and too many consumers. In a broad way, this
formula was correct, and remedies for the situation, though
slow and difficult, were not beyond hope. But the *Tableau économique*, abstract and theoretical though it was, never was allowed to achieve any circulation worth mentioning. It was
printed up in an edition of just three copies, never circulated,
never debated, never even considered as a practical expedient
or a guide to action. Quesnay's ideas, which fell on stony
ground in France, showed their basic vitality when picked up
by Adam Smith for incorporation in *The Wealth of Nations* and

then put into practice by William Pitt the younger. But in France they remained the deadest of dead letters.

In the long run, increasing the number of producers may have been a major part of the answer to France's economic problems; in the short run, an equally valid solution would have been to widen the tax base, by taxing the exempt and privileged classes. The upper clergy, very wealthy, had long been exempt from all taxation, though occasionally they might make a voluntary donation. The nobility paid none of the lesser taxes and consistently managed to evade the basic *vingtième*, which was supposed to fall alike on all. The obvious remedy was a new land tax from which nobody, whether cleric or aristocrat, would be exempt and a sharply increased stamp tax which also would fall on everybody. In January of 1787, Charles de Calonne proposed these new steps to an Assembly of Notables, specially convened to consider the state of the realm. In substance, he was proposing nothing but what Turgot and Necker had advised before. But in order to justify the new impositions, he had to explain the real financial situation of the kingdom. Apparently Necker's very gratifying *Compte rendu* of 1781, showing a neat surplus of ten million livres, had been based on estimates and expectations, not realities; the actual deficit for 1781 had been in the neighborhood of 46 million livres. For 1787 the fearless minister estimated a deficit of over 112 million livres. He suffered the usual fate of those who bring bad tidings; the deficits were blamed on him, and when he had been dismissed and exiled, the Notables anticipated there would be no further nonsense about taxing the privileged.

They were of course mistaken. Calonne's successor, the conservative cleric Loménie de Brienne, urged exactly the same policies on exactly the same grounds. The financial crisis did not disappear with the departure of "Monsieur Deficit." Brienne also made clear to Louis XVI (to whom things had to be made *very* clear) that the royal budget must be trimmed. And the king did try. He sold some town houses, reduced his hunting establishment (over the insolent objections of the hunt master), streamlined the postal service, and went to work on the swollen pension list. Established pensions were cut (the fattest first), future pensions were limited, multiple pensions (often concealed under special names, such as *gratifications* or *traitements*) were cancelled. The army, top-heavy with general officers, was advised to reduce numbers as fast as possible. All these reforms were steps in the right direction, but they came very late, and they were minor in relation to the dimensions of the problem, whether one defined that problem fiscally or socially.

In fact, the reforms, feeble as they were, sometimes served simply to reinforce basic inequities in the system. Since the military establishment guarding the court was too elaborate and expensive, the Gendarmes de la Garde were abolished outright and the Gardes du Corps subjected to a modest reduction. Nobody even pretended it was a coincidence that the first group consisted entirely of nonaristocrats, the second group entirely of young nobles. Routine procedure in the old army had been that a young nobleman was appointed captain and within a couple of years automatically promoted—with or without merit—to colonel; reforms somewhat extended the period of apprenticeship, to make certain that the new colonel knew the rudiments of his trade—but simultaneously made promotion beyond the rank of major almost inconceivable for anyone not an aristocrat. (As for the lower ranks, refusal to recognize merit there is written large in the biographies of Napoleon's generals. Hoche, Marceau, Masséna, Ney, Murat, Soult, T. A. Dumas—only one of them rose as high as sergeant, and most remained private soldiers until a

career open to their talents transformed them, almost over-
night, into the most daring and skilled staff of generals in Europe.)

While the king wrestled to cut expenses, often against
the direct obstruction of his wealthy and privileged subjects,
those wealthy and privileged classes, as represented in the
Parlement de Paris, meditated imposing taxation on themselves. But they did not meditate very hard; their minds had
long been made up, and they had an easy escape route to hand.
Taxation, they said, did not lie in their jurisdiction; new taxes
could be imposed only by the States General. Technically,
perhaps they were partly right, but their good faith is open to
serious question, if only because on other occasions they
never showed the slightest inclination to self-sacrifice or even
to cooperation with the administration. For example, Necker
in 1781 had asked for an accounting, from all recent benefi-
ciaries of the king's "generosity," of what they had and how
they got it. Clearly he suspected (and in fact with justice) that
they had been plundering the monarch they were ostensibly
serving. Fewer than one in thirty of the profiteers even both-
ered to respond, and though the request was renewed seven
years later, nothing ever came of it. Men thus hardened to
barefaced jobbery would not be likely to view with open minds
the question of taxing themselves. When the Parlement de
Paris rejected Brienne's last modest gestures toward fiscal reform—too little and too late as they were—that tipped the
balance. The king had to try bypassing or overruling the
Parlement; that constituted the basic legal conflict leading to
the convocation of the States General, and from there on, ac-
celerating with terrifying speed, the arc of the *ancien régime*
turned steadily downward.

Avarice may have been largely responsible for the aristocracy's flat rejection of reform; it is hard to think they would

have had much trouble with the legal technicalities if their self-interest had been as deeply involved for reform as it was against it. But the aristocrats sitting in the Parlement de Paris were moved, as well, by political pressures from outside their own social order. Nobody outside the royal family wanted to see the monarchy financially secure on the basis of the *status quo*. (The aristocrats should have, but were too blind to recognize their own interest.) Reforms of some sort were needed; to get them on the table, organs and agents of opinion far removed from the aristocracy were willing to support even the Parlement de Paris. Tocqueville saw the situation clearly. "This new and irregular power of opinion," he wrote, "found in the Parlement the only tool it could use; it laid hold of that tool, not to make the Parlement powerful, not because it was the most popular body, but because it was the only body in France well enough organized, large and strong enough, to stand up against the royal power, and shake the establishment that people really wanted to overthrow."*

Fundamentally, however, it is a very bourgeois judgment that represents the aristocracy of the old regime as either avaricious or stupid. The traditions in which they were reared made of selfishness not an individual vice but a class duty, and total ignorance of the lower orders a matter of elementary good taste. Narrowing a little the context in which they are

---

*Tocqueville, *L'Ancien Régime et la révolution*, II, 103, ed. André Jardin. Who exactly used whom, as between the Parlement and public opinion, is a hard point. So far as it could, the Parlement masqueraded as a libertarian force. In the declaration of May 3, 1788, it not only declared that taxes could be voted only by the States General, but added that *lettres de cachet* were illegal and that the customs and privileges of the separate provinces were inviolable. Linking these issues, it put the onus of oppression on the central government; while seeming to appeal for the rights of the individual, its real intent was simply to preserve the privileges of the privileged.

viewed, one might well say that the aristocrats of the old regime expressed their decadence, not in weakness, but in a fresh access of strength and confidence. That was what made them think themselves independent of the monarch, the bureaucracy, and the third estate, all at once. Their whole mystique was antibourgeois, antiprudential; if they had been able even to comprehend the dangers they ran from the third estate (including those gaunt, ragged skulkers in the backwoods whom they had never encountered, even in dreams), they would not have been that hermetic, self-sufficient corporation which, simply as a piece of social engineering, had to be destroyed. Being so entire to themselves, they could only be reasoned with in one way. Perhaps it is true, as some have thought, that the *charte* of 1814, which compromised at least for a while the issues of the revolution, could very well have been had in 1789, without a quarter-century of blood, agony, and bitterness. But if this is true at all, it is true only in a narrow, legalistic sense. The code of the aristocrats, the code of those who had learned to hate and mistrust aristocrats, could not have been satisfied with a compromise. Human materials had to be modified, and the aristocrats, as the most obsolete class, modified most.* In the measure that we can see them as decadent, it was their imperviousness that made them so. The government's

---

*It is true that some aristocrats involved themselves in industry. As landowners, they often became mine owners in spite of themselves, and then mill owners because they had loose money to invest. Some owned plantations in the colonies, and a few, hiding behind pseudonyms, even became sleeping partners in retail trade operations. But these were ways of milking the monopoly they shared with the upper bourgeoisie. Large dowries accompanying bourgeois brides when they married noblemen were another recognized way of replenishing depleted family coffers. But were these roughly equivalent devices sufficient to transform a basically parasitic to a dynamic class? Some revisionist historians have attempted the argument, but not very persuasively.

financial problems were not the heart of the matter. Governments have been known to declare bankruptcy, reorganize,
and pull out of their difficulties. But the attitude of "don't
know and don't care" on the part of society's most privileged
classes was deadly. It is an attitude to which two-tier economies, such as we seem to be developing in the United States,
are evidently liable. The French experience adds callousness
at home to the Roman example of weakness abroad as suggestive evidence of imminent social decline, and so of potential
decadence.

THE ROMANOVS: HISTORY AS BLACK FARCE

Before 1789, the French nation was almost spectacularly innocent of any revolutionary ideologies. The chief modern example of a social revolution, the English commonwealth of the
seventeenth century, was so alien that Robespierre himself in
a patriotic speech could rail against Cromwell as a tyrant and
usurper equivalent to Caesar. Within French society there
were few preliminary threats, no abortive coups, no flashing
signal lights of popular disaffection. The regime did not lose
a major war (the Seven Years' War had been concluded a
quarter-century before); there were no major disputes over
the succession. The revolution struck like lightning from a
clear blue sky. After the French example, of course, that sort
of naïve assurance was never possible again. During the great
English agitations over the Reform Bill of 1832, it was the
threat of working-class revolts on the French model that was
most effective in moving the grumbling, reluctant House of
Lords to give its sullen consent. Few of the Lords were convinced in their hearts that the old system needed reforming.
Most of them, in addition, feared that a first yielding to popular pressure would lead to a second and a third. They were

absolutely right. The first reform bill led not only to the second and third but to Chartist agitations, Corn Law reforms, and to that numbing moment in 1911 when the Lords voted themselves, as an active element in the constitutional process, out of existence. All this was implicit in the 1832 vote, and much of it the Lords foresaw truly. Yet yield they did, having in the back of their minds the fate of the French *émigrés*; and if the *émigrés* had had such an instructive example before their eyes, they too might have bowed to the storm before it uprooted them. Why the regime of the Romanovs, with a century and a quarter to read the record of history, did not do so to their own better advantage is a question more curious than profitable. From stupidity there is always something to be learned, but it's always the same thing: don't be stupid.

The last five Romanovs were self-proclaimed autocrats, ruling over a discontented population that had been demanding representative institutions at least since the Decembrist conspiracy of 1825. The institution of a Duma or representative assembly, scornfully rejected for eighty years, was granted only in 1905, after the defeat by Japan and the revolt it triggered, when its granting had to be read as a sign of weakness, not generosity. Having been granted, it was then robbed of all substantial reality in a way to convince everyone of the Czar's pusillanimity and bad faith. For decades national minorities throughout the empire had been restless and discontented; for centuries, the miserable lot of serfs, peasants, derelicts, and the lower orders generally had expressed itself in savage riots and mutinies—spontaneous, unorganized, brutal, and just as brutally repressed. The czarist regime, so oppressive that it would have been absolutely intolerable had it not been so grotesquely inefficient, systematically sapped the lifeblood and abused the docility of its citizens.

By the twentieth century the autocracy was old; it car-

ried on its back many of the sins of previous ages—the duplicity of Alexander I, the frozen imbecilities of Nicholas I,
the cruel repressions of Alexanders II and III. There had
been Romanovs on the throne of Russia since 1613. A few of
them had occasionally taken the trouble to camouflage authoritarian attitudes behind liberal words and gestures. But
mostly their record was written by the knout, the police spy,
the hangman, and the long, bloody trail leading to the drifts
of Siberia. The Romanovs were not simply reactionary after
the fashion of monarchs who hold to strict principles. They
demanded unquestioning obedience, not to what they stood
for unconditionally, but to their whim of the moment. It was a
Romanov who forbade his people to discuss the conduct of
government affairs, even to praise it: they should not, he said,
think of such matters at all. This was the burden of history
inherited by Nicholas II, which he did nothing to shift or dis-
own. His regime was not only politically and economically
backward, it knew itself to be such, it gloried in the fact, and
thought anybody who was ashamed of it must be afflicted with
diabolic possession.

Of all the Romanovs, Nicholas II was the weakest and
most pretentious*; he was also the one called upon to face the
most difficult and explosive problems. These were areas of
technical backwardness, in the first place—a vast rural vil-
lage-economy, still farming in the medieval manner; illiteracy,
drunkenness, bad roads, poor communications, corrupt and
incompetent officials, a tax system as regressive as any in prerevolutionary France or the lower Roman empire. This ramshackle structure was subjected to new and special strains

---

*Trying hard to say something nice about a fellow-monarch, Kaiser Wil-
helm remarked that Nicholas wasn't treacherous, just weak; weakness, he
added, was not treachery, but fulfilled all its functions. The comparison
with Louis XVI cries out to be made.

when foreign capitalists, eager to exploit cheap Russian labor, recruited peasants by the thousands to sweat in barracks-factories for subsistence wages. An oppressive and regularly unsuccessful military establishment, bigoted racial practices, and a cruel system of internal exile, convict labor camps, and surveillance by secret police fill out the picture. But just as dangerous to the regime as any of these weak spots, and doubtless the consequence of some of them, was a widely supported and deeply entrenched conspiratorial and insurrectionary organization, implacably devoted to overthrowing the Czar and his rule. The myth of the revolution, of its inevitability, of its apocalyptic glories, was well established in Russian thought long before the publication of *The Communist Manifesto*. Messianic Marxism built on a foundation of Russian messianic expectations; between them, they would have made the position of Nicholas II an uneasy one, had he been wise as Solomon.

None of the Romanovs ever reminded anyone of King Solomon; indeed, it can be said with some justice that the strength with which the radical left was able to destroy the autocracy was bestowed on it by the autocracy itself. Czarist opposition to change, and even to the discussion of change,* was so ferocious that nothing but conspiracy remained; and in conspiracies it's obvious what tempers soon come to prevail.

---

*Of Nicholas I, who ruled from 1825 to 1855, years during which the face of western Europe was utterly transformed, it has been said that his reign has no history at all; things happened from time to time, but in the sense of development or even a consistent tendency, there was nothing. Uvarov, minister of education in 1833, publicly declared that it would be his policy, if he could possibly do it, to retard the development of Russia by fifty years. But compared with his successor Shikhmatov, Uvarov has been called "a paladin of enlightenment." Edward Crankshaw, *The Shadow of the Winter Palace* (New York: Viking, 1976).

Decadent Societies

An autocratic regime behaves autocratically—even in occasionally doing good, it cannot help doing itself harm. The emancipation of the serfs in 1861, a measure enlightened in itself, was carried out by Alexander II in such a way as to ensure him a maximum of ill will from all concerned. The serfs themselves were burdened with "redemption payments" for fifty years into the future, were granted particles of land too small to support them, were saddled with a great burden of national taxation,* and were so effectively barred from education that most peasants could learn reading and arithmetic only when dragooned into the army. As for the provincial gentry, their most generous and respectful requests—to be allowed to help with the reforms, to be permitted to share in the burden of taxation—were brutally rejected and the authors rewarded with prison terms. The Czar alone would do the reforming, if reform there was to be. He was supported in this blind resolve by the bureaucracy, jealous of its privileged position, and by the big landowners, fearful that lesser landowners might dominate a popular assembly. But really the Czar needed no support; his own decision to make all decisions was sufficient. Thus he forced even conservatives into reluctant sympathy with revolutionaries, or covert admiration of them, such as clings to half-outlaw figures like Bazarov and Raskolnikov. After the 1881 assassination of Alexander II by bomb-throwing anarchists, the dynasty ruled almost entirely through the agency of the secret police—a practice with an ugly modern heritage that needs no emphasis.

---

*In 1895 it was estimated that for the same piece of land a peasant would pay twice as much in direct taxes as a nobleman; in addition, most indirect taxation also fell on the peasantry because such taxes were levied on the staples of life and (under the guise of morality) on liquor, of which peasants were the chief consumers.

France and Russia

Secret Agents

From the early days of Bakunin and Herzen, the Russian revolutionary movement regularly supported in their several exiles nests of voluble sectarian theorists. The government did not much mind their going abroad, sometimes connived at their departure, and (at least in the case of Herzen) read their fulminations with some interest. Less welcome were the invisible cells of underground conspirators within Russia, combinations of agitators, propagandists, assassins, and perpetrators of symbolic outrages. Some of the recruits to these groups were people with special grievances: women, because they were excluded from the universities; Jews, because the government tolerated when it did not actually encourage pogroms; serfs or former serfs, in whom still rankled the bitterness of slavery imperfectly and grudgingly reformed; members of national minority groups. But increasingly they were joined by alienated young people of the middle classes, natural organizers, bureaucrats, and functionaries, for whom the revolutionary motive may have been nothing more than rage at the stupid inefficiency of the system. Most of these young people got their real education at the hands of the Czar's crafty and unscrupulous police, and a harsh process of learning it was. As treachery bred treachery, so terror fed on terror; in their secret running battle with the police, the revolutionaries grew steadily more calculating and conspiratorial— more convinced, too, that the Czar's government was sustained only by gangs as unscrupulous as themselves. The last years of the last Czar's reign were marked by a steady string of assassinations, peasant risings and barn burnings, strikes and sabotage, along with a steady counterfire of executions, exiles, espionage, counterespionage, and the hateful activity of *agents provocateurs*. Meanwhile, the conspirators abroad published and quarreled, calculated and waited. When the regime stumbled and staggered in 1905, they were at it at once, to bring it down; when the Germans wanted to finish it off in the spring of 1917, they introduced Lenin, like a deadly microbe, riding in a sealed train across Europe to do the job for which he had trained all his life.

To the revolutionary ideology that Lenin carried with him to the Finland station there is no need to attribute supernatural powers. No government in the world's history was more rotten-ripe for collapse than that of Nicholas II; none contributed more lavishly to its own destruction. By the time Lenin left Zurich, the Czar was for all practical purposes out of his mind, and no force on earth could save his rule. In its conflicts with Mensheviks and Socialist Revolutionaries, the Bolshevik faction won out for simple, practical reasons: it was better organized, more unified. It profited also from the unanimous agreement of all the political parties, including the Constitutional Democrats (Cadets), that the old regime must be, not just reformed, but destroyed and replaced. This was a real triumph of long-continued propaganda—perhaps a tribute, as well, to the Czar's power of exciting universal mistrust and loathing. But the path of the Bolsheviks to power was much eased when the Cadets blithely took their stand with "the broad masses," never so much as inquiring who the leaders of those broad masses were going to be. Even a respectable history teacher like Milyukov felt safe in refusing to cooperate with the weakened Czarist government on certain reform measures (last-minute, but not entirely unpromising) because he was unable to recognize any danger to his constitutional liberalism from the left. At the last moment, when the infatuate Czar was able to recognize a little of *his* imminent danger, the people who might have rescued him from it were unable to recognize their own.

The resilient, indestructible energy of the Russian people under the weight of a government that was worse than inert can hardly be exaggerated. Nicholas in the last years of his misrule received not only more support than he deserved but a bouquet of achievements that might have redeemed any rule but his. The explosive, multifarious flowering of Russian culture in music, art, and poetry has already been mentioned. The minister Stolypin, harsh, hateful, and hated as few men have ever been, nonetheless engineered a program of genuine agricultural reform, establishing a class of independent and progressive peasant proprietors numbering in the millions. What he did was simply free them from the village communes, where their work was tied to the pace of the slowest, weakest, and most backward. It was, as Stolypin put it, a gamble, not on the drunk and the feeble but on the sober and the strong—who also happened to be the ruthless and the greedy. Their nickname, "kulaks," means "fists"; as a class of producers, they were so successful that the Bolsheviks had to exterminate them *en masse*, and what the history of Russia would be like had they been created as little as twenty-five years earlier one can scarcely imagine. (With all its many shortcomings, Czarist Russia was a massive exporter of grain; why the Soviet Union, with all its vaunted technology, falls chronically short of meeting its own need for the staples is plainly not one but many questions.) For his pains in creating this one strong prop of the tottering regime he served, Stolypin was assassinated, by a Social Revolutionary to be sure, but not without strong suspicion of government complicity in the deed. That would have been Nicholas's style. In much the same way, he used Witte and Kokovtsev to negotiate French loans, then kicked them out and replaced them with the idiot Goremykin. Between 1905 and 1917 the several Dumas, after preliminary flounderings, did some good work to establish representative government, but they were hamstrung by the bureaucracy and the autocrat, in addition to being boycotted by the extreme left.

After the early years of disaster in the great war, the volunteer patriotism of the *zemstvos* (district and provincial councils) did something to organize the nation—though they had all been told, rudely and firmly, that their help was not wanted. The armies themselves, after their staggering defeats in Prussia, rallied with futile bravery and even a semblance of efficiency to carry the war against the Austrians. Given their sickening casualties and the total inadequacy of their behind-the-lines support, no other armies in the world would have stuck it out so stubbornly.

Still, the old regime fell, as it deserved to fall; the reasons for its falling, in spite of a long-suffering people and immense material resources, are obvious enough to make irrelevant most of the lessons that the Russian experience scrawled crudely across the much-scribbled wall of history. Make men desperate, and they will sooner or later revolt; deprive them of any stake in existing society, and they will pin their hopes on another. Neglect their welfare scandalously, and they will learn to neglect yours. Drive your potential friends and protectors into the arms of your worst enemies, and you will be left naked to the storm. Don't go to war when your armies are weak, your people disunited, your goals unclear, and your enemy strong. Such copybook maxims for rulers need no recitation. A little more complex are the lessons taught by the Russian revolutionaries. Much of the groundwork for their success was laid by hammering home two or three simple ideas, which they found the liberal *intelligentsia** unable to re-

---

*Though often applied to groups in other countries, the word "intelligentsia" properly describes a peculiarly Russian phenomenon. A few isolated "thinkers" adrift in a sea of illiterates, deliberately deprived of social functions and practical experience, but given self-importance by the mere fact of education, they were noses of wax, easily twisted by anyone who thought it worth his while.

sist. When they were able, with the Czar's help, to persuade their fellow travellers that reform accomplished nothing, and so a revolution was inevitable, half their work was done; those who foresaw the future so confidently must naturally be able to control and direct it, must possess proprietary rights in it. The old regime was decadent, good for nothing but fertilizer, out of which the seeds of a new society could grow. From this it followed naturally that the best and most hopeful features of the old regime should be ruthlessly destroyed, the worst features preserved for propaganda advantage. Reform was bad especially when it was good; not for the first or last time, the relation between extreme right and extreme left proved to be symbiotic.

A particular advantage for the radical propagandists, though only a temporary one, was that their ideal had not yet been given form and so was not easy to criticize. Had anyone foreseen the famines that followed "liquidation" of the kulaks, the purges of Stalin, or the ongoing, apparently permanent, existence of the Gulag Archipelago, the propaganda task of the Bolsheviks would have been much more difficult. But of course foresight is not given to man. Socialism came into being as the culmination of generations of liberal and libertarian thought and there was no way of knowing when it would turn into its own dialectical opposite. Nicholas II was as much deluded as anyone. He opposed the revolutionaries because he thought them exponents of freedom; had he enjoyed foresight, he might have welcomed them as a more powerful but not very different version of autocracy.

Three of the four decadent societies so far mentioned clearly fall into a group: the Roman west, the old regime in France, and the Romanov dynasty. They were all dominated by exclusive, elite groups, unable or unwilling to persuade the "lower orders" that they too had a stake in the society. They resisted domestic reforms and uniformly put the heavy burdens of maintaining and defending society on the poor, while reserving the social advantages for the upper crust. All three societies were in deep financial trouble before their downfall; all three showed strong symptoms of tax exhaustion. None of the three made any serious effort to examine or analyze their predicament; none tried to project a vision of the future, except as more of the same. Though in different ways, all three put into the hands of their enemies the weapons by which they themselves would perish: the Romans by yielding up their swords to the Ostrogoths, the French aristos by calling for the States General, the Czarist autocracy by demonstrating, all but conclusively, that only a revolution which demolished it could make a significant change. All three, though they had long histories and strong traditions, went down very quickly.

A certain amount of debauchery and randy free-wheeling characterized all three societies, but nobody has proposed that it was peculiar to them or significantly influenced their downfalls. The normal human failings of sloth and cowardice, greed and jealousy made themselves felt in the decadent, as they commonly do in nondecadent societies. Depopulation was not a problem; the fields were not exhausted, nor had the mines been depleted. Defeat in battle was at most a contributory cause in Russia; in Rome, it appeared a consequence of other causes and in France was only remote and secondary. No, the malady, if malady there was, lay in the social order, and a striking circumstance demonstrates it. After the French and Russian revolutions, the new societies displayed a tremendous outburst of exuberant, dynamic energy. In the nature of things, such outbursts cannot last very long, and they sometimes occur without the special stimulus of a revolution; both France and Russia were overdue for large-scale industrialization; it is easy to assign to revolution as such more credit than it deserves. Still, in these two instances the turnabout was striking. The armies of Napoleon, which threw back invaders, crushed opponents, and for twenty-five years marched like giants back and forth across Europe, consisted almost entirely of men born under the *ancien régime*. They were led by officers for whom the royal establishment had never been able to find more than menial positions. The industrial machine that backed them up was animated by the new ideal of a *carrière ouverte aux talents*; a new legal code went far beyond anything envisioned by Turgot or Quesnay in unleashing the productive energies of the nation. So too with the industrial and military powers of the USSR; by rights they should have been utterly exhausted when the new regime came to power. After the frightful slaughter of the imperialist war, the wars of intervention, the civil wars, despite domestic terror, despotism, ill-conceived planning, and downright famine, the Soviets were able to free their territory and build on it, in very short order, an industrial plant second only to one. The armies that threw back Hitler at Stalingrad and converged for the kill at Berlin redeemed in full those that perished like cattle at Tannenberg. As much as anything else, the energies of the postrevolutionary regime defined the decadence of the prerevolutionary one.

Byzantium, though it stands in many respects with the three decadent societies—an oligarchy of priests and soldiers, severe, unyielding, topheavy—was yet different enough to have had an instructively different history. It was a sea-based, an Aegean, and very much a commercial empire. Trade, from the Black Sea, from the Orient, from Egypt and Russia, was its life breath; and in the nature of things a commercial oligarchy, where fortunes can be made or lost on a single venture, is more flexible than one based on land-tenure. As a rule, Byzantium did not try to dominate land masses, except economically; its power bases were islands or ports along the seacoasts. It therefore had fewer peasants to oppress, and oppressed them less cruelly. Byzantium was a multiracial community, and it used the advantages, besides enduring the disadvantages, of that option; one of its favorite devices for assimilating an enemy (like the inconvenient Bulgars, for example) was to admit some of its leaders to the Byzantine aristocracy. Even the empire's rulers often came from the outside: Justinian was an Illyrian, his queen Theodora came from Cappadocia, and the so-called Macedonian Dynasty that followed them was in fact Armenian. These leaders were quick to learn from the errors and from the successes of their rivals; the pattern of their recruiting and strategic doctrines shows a consistent effort at economy in the use of violence that could be called "modern" if it were not also in the highest degree Machiavellian.

For these and no doubt for other reasons, the Byzantines maintained their resilience during a decline that was so long and slow, broken by so many partial recoveries and resourceful adaptations that one dare not call the whole process "decadence." Its peculiar history prepares one for the equally peculiar development of what was called, for a surprisingly short period of time, the empire of Great Britain.

The British Empire

The slow expansion of the British Empire and its bumpy subsidence through a series of military triumphs, economic defeats, and deliberate divestitures can only be compared with the trajectory of Byzantium. Enormous differences are apparent in the magnitude of the imperial complex, the relative proportions of persuasion and compulsion, the shifting patterns of alliance, the very different roles of technology. But before such contrasts can even be attempted, it behooves us to ask whether Britain really had an empire at all. In the early days, at least, the nation was very far from building or even intending an empire in the marketplace sense of the word—many subjects, much tribute, centralized political control. Most of her early and gradual acquisitions were either trading posts in coastal cities or scattered strong points, mostly insular, where her navy could put in for information, refitting, and resupply. Up to and including the Seven Years' War (1756–1763), the wars in which England established her world position were trade wars but hardly wars of territorial acquisition. Sir John Seeley once said, with a seriousness that German scholarship is quite incapable of understanding, that the British Empire was acquired in a fit of absentmindedness. In fact the early stages of British expansion show few marks of deliberate intent.

The three major land masses where the empire came to command large numbers of people were North America, India, and Australia; as they were acquired by different procedures, for different purposes, and involved radically different populations, Britain adopted a different tactic and terminology for each. The broad lines of differentiation are too familiar to need more than sketching out.

In India, where commerce was the original driving motive, British power in the indirect form of the East India Company lurked in large measure behind native rulers. Since they took command of ancient autocracies, the British, even while milking the land of its wealth, could readily cast themselves in the role of civilizing and moderating influences. In trying to abolish suttee (widow-incineration) and the worst excesses of the caste system, they did what any Western power must have done; and in trying to provide for India major material projects like railway lines, universities, newspapers, the rudiments of a sanitary code, and the basic substructures of a civil service and representative government, they contributed largely to the making of a nation that had to be made this way, whether it was to be "theirs" or not. A scarcely deliberate contribution to Indian unity was adoption of the English language; a nation with 147 different vernaculars is ungovernable, unless its people share a common second language. For India that language is firmly fixed as English. Yet for all these contributions to Indian development, the British presence in India was always that of a "superior" race, exploiting even as it (by its own lights) benefited the "inferior" one. The color barrier was very hard to cross; Victorian evangelical Christianity threw up fearful obstacles to easy communication with "pagans"; and the advent of Gandhi, with his long-sustained and terribly effective program of passive resistance, posed for the British occupiers problems they were quite unable to solve. The simple fact is that, with rare exceptions for special individuals and special occasions, the British never established themselves in India except as intruders; here they were real imperialists. They held on as long as they could, under shifting pretexts, but essentially by force; and when force failed, after World War II, their departure was abrupt.

Quite different was the record in North America, where the British came first as traders, trappers, and settlers, hardly at all as exploiters of the native populations. True, they drove away the aborigines and conquered the French Canadians, with consequences being felt to this day. Occasionally, the colonies were used as a dumping ground for sectarian troublemakers or criminals; very often their development was slanted in directions favorable to the mother country. Control of one continent from another was bound to be irksome in the days when asking a question in Philadelphia and getting an answer from Whitehall might consume as much as six months. The men who came to the American colonies naturally tended to be rough, impatient, independent fellows; they could not be kept indefinitely in leading-strings. During the long period of indifference and mutual neglect for which Sir Robert Walpole's government was originally responsible, the two parties learned to jog along comfortably enough without noticing one another too closely.

The Seven Years' War (known in America as the French and Indian War) put an end to that by forcing the English to ask the Americans kindly to contribute to the cost of their own defence and not to go adventuring beyond the Alleghenies, where they might stir up another war. The struggle that broke out in 1776 thus ratified a slow separation that had already established itself *de facto*, and it is significant that even at the time a substantial party in England sympathized with the Americans, seeing in their struggle against George III parallels with the seventeenth-century struggle against Charles I. Thus it appears that the chief American colonies began slipping out of any possible imperial scheme even before they had been properly integrated in it; and at the very height of empire-building, a strong party in England thought (for reasons good and bad, as it happened) that forcing men of English stock into associations against their will was incompatible with English liberties. As applied to Great Britain, one may recall, the use of the word "empire" was about a hundred years in the future when the American Revolution broke out. Colonies, yes; obviously the North Americans were colonists of Great Britain, but an empire, with its connotations of one-man, divine-right rule, was offensive to a people brought up on catchwords like "the liberty of the subject." A voluntary association with America everyone approved of; but a voluntary empire is not an empire at all.

Canada and Australia show how easily and naturally components of the "empire" where the imperialist element was weak to start with drifted imperceptibly into dominion status and then toward total independence. Exploitation of a colony can of course take many forms, and in the early days undesirables and incompetents were shipped off to Australia and Canada, as to the embryo United States. But during the latter part of the nineteenth century, public-interest groups and semi-official agencies began actively encouraging emigration to the colonies by capable and ambitious Englishmen of all sorts. This was not empire-building in the usual sense; the emigrants were not sent in groups, they had no official status or ties, they were not being posted to garrisons. No doubt it was expected that when they achieved wealth and influence in their new homes, they would remember fondly the land of their origins. But the Manchester school of economics, which made a fetish of free trade, welcomed the notion of imperial federalism, and one path to federalism lay through free emigration. During the mid-nineteenth century, the mother country held an unbreakable monopoly on the processes and machinery and lines of credit by which raw materials from colonies and ex-colonies could be converted to finished goods; she also dominated the carrying industry. It was a period when England was exporting capital liberally to the colonies; by exporting men too, on the most liberal conceivable terms, she strengthened, rather than weakened, her position. The ideal was a set of mini-Britains around the world, stimulated by the flow of British capital, trained to British institutions, selling predominantly to British markets, yielding a nice profit to British investors.* The aborigines of Australia and Canada, not to mention the French Canadians, did not promise to develop satisfactorily along these lines and so tended to be shunted aside; British liberties were limited, not infrequently, to those who had earned them by taking pains to be born of British stock. The British record was blotched at best, and sometimes its "best" amounted to no more than letting local magnates take the blame for some rather dirty work. Yet the objective was not, as a rule, to bind the possessions in chains of steel. For a while at least, and in some parts of the world more than others, the vision of association under tutelage developing toward political independence tempered by cultural sympathy was not beyond hope. In the light of this aspiration (which, naturally, was not everybody's, but for periods of significant time exercised broad influence), the "decline" of the

---

*To this day, one hears, the last outposts of empire in Gibraltar and Hong Kong preserve a set of imperial values and a measure of imperial devotion surprising to visitors from the home islands, where things aren't always so *pukka.*

British empire, that is, the independence of its composite elements, merges imperceptibly into the process of its "rise" and can actually be seen as its culminating achievement. Contrariwise, when organic, absentminded growth began hardening at the end of the nineteenth century into an aggressive doctrine, an acute observer might have suspected that the system was developing hardening of the arteries, or coming under attack from outside, or both.

Territorial acquisition was a small part of British foreign policy, witness the meager results, in real-estate terms, of her twenty-year participation, between 1795 and 1815, in the wars against Napoleon. A few scattered islands, of which Malta and Trinidad were the most important, and a foothold on the Cape of Good Hope (not yet known as gold and diamond country)—that was all. Of course Britain gained plenty of compensating advantages elsewhere, but this casualness about picking up territories complements an equal casualness about letting them go. The Americans fought for their independence; the Australians and Canadians gained about as much, only more slowly. Their gains were made, not just when the empire was being dismantled under pressure of economic necessity, but as a result of spontaneous development, only gently resisted and sometimes actually seconded by the home country. Britain turned to the monolithic imperialist formula only late in its history, only for a short period of time, for rather specific purposes, and by no means with the unanimous support of its people. A crucial date is 1876, when Disraeli generated for the gratification of Queen Victoria the title "Empress of India." Its adoption was sharply criticized at home, and defended on the cautious grounds that it was an Indian title, for use in India only, to impress Indians who were used to such fulsome terminology. Less than a quarter-century later, Rudyard Kipling was writing a "Recessional" for the empire, and the bloom had rubbed off the imperialist ideal.

Obviously the empire, such as it became, had been a long time growing before 1876, and took a somewhat shorter time to subside after 1902. What helped turn its development from one direction to the other was a linked chain of challenges, in the form of trade and manufacturing competition as well as direct military rivalry. Having long had a practical monopoly of advanced work in textiles and metallurgy, Britain came under pressure, at a time when her industrial plant was aging, from more up-to-date factories in Germany and America. Already there is a major difference to be underlined: none of the societies previously discussed had to cope with rivals who were technologically superior. Not only Britain's enemies but her allies and former colonies undermined her position. Instead of being consumers, as heretofore, nations like Canada, Australia, and America became competing suppliers, aided, often enough, by the possession of productive machinery originally made in England. Further pressure rose from a flood of cheap grain from the American prairies, carried on new American railroads and new ocean-going steamers. These grain imports, unrestrained by protective tariffs because of Britain's free-trade policies, devastated British agriculture and made the nation more dependent than ever on foreign markets for her manufactured goods, just when those markets were shrinking. Under these threatening circumstances, the safest British markets appeared to be the various components of the empire. They were also the places where British credits could most safely be extended and British investments placed. In the long run, to be sure, the colonies aided by British credits would begin competing with British industry. But, starting in the late nineteenth century, this prospect was so little feared that English investment abroad amounted regularly (and sometimes by a very large margin) to more than English investment in domestic production. Greater dependence of England on her imperial possessions led naturally to an increasingly aggressive tone in British imperial policy after 1870.

A new military fact also sharpened the stridency of England's imperial pretensions toward the end of the 19th century; this was the rise of Germany to preeminence in Europe as a result of the Franco-Prussian war of 1870. That encounter was brief and terribly decisive; as a result of it, France could no longer effectively stand up to Germany, so that England had to do more herself to maintain the balances on which her foreign policy had long rested. Confrontation with the blunt and outspoken Germans produced exaggerated responses of jingoism and racism in England herself, and even protecting the status quo led inevitably to further expansion. To take a single instance: a French company under de Lesseps had been the original builders of the Suez Canal (1869), though of course with a great deal of international capital and the blessing of the Egyptian "government," such as it was. Disraeli's 1875 purchase of shares in the canal corporation from that spectacular scoundrel the Khedive Ismail was certainly a prudent and far-sighted move. With so many possessions and responsibilities in the east, Britain could ill afford the risk of having to send her ships back and forth around the Cape of Good Hope. By the same token, she could not allow the stridently aggressive Germans (whose loans to Egypt were in standing default) to control the canal. But the French, whose interest in the canal was by far the greatest, were paralyzed with fear as a result of the 1870 war. As they could or would do nothing to stop the Germans (whose alliance with the Turks made them a present danger), the British had, in effect, to take over Egypt themselves. And "taking over" Egypt meant, inevitably, taking over a tangle of troubles, with the slave trade, with the insurrectionary mahdi, with independence movements in the Sudan.

Thus in the years before World War I, the British were pushed, some of them less reluctantly than others, toward a more aggressive imperialist stance than they had assumed before. And while, within the narrow family of European nations, the Germans blamed the English for their crass monopoly of markets and the English blamed the Germans for their aggressive drive after markets, both nations were the half-conscious victims of the United States, which was already in process of catching and overtaking them in its drive for industrial development and markets of its own.

DRY ROT

Any social structure which has stood without major alteration for a couple of hundred years is, on the face of it, mature; nothing alters the fact of time. But the diagnosis of decadence must rest on anomalies and rigidities in the structure of society, over which determined men with clear minds might have exercised some control. Historical hindsight gives us a generous advantage in such matters, which we cannot be shy about using. For one simple thing, obsolescence of the British industrial plant (a fact of life to which economists and social planners were calling attention as much as a century ago) was not an inevitable, immutable process. During the late nineteenth century, major steps were taken to improve British housing, education, local government, and conditions of public health. That there should have been no systematic effort to update the industrial machine or to subsidize the expensive shift toward creation of new products at a time when the na-

tion's welfare depended so heavily on foreign sales was a notable piece of social blindness.*

Revamping an entire industrial plant already in existence may be too much to expect of any society not threatened
with deadly peril; brutally defeated nations like Germany and
Japan are the best modern instances of total reconstruction.
But in the late nineteenth century, a few practical steps to
stimulate technical innovation would not have been beyond
Britain's capacity—as they are not presently beyond our own.
Research and development provide small-scale models for industrial reconstruction; academic laboratories can provide
useful stimuli. The inventions of the eighteenth and early
nineteenth century, which made England proverbial for mechanical ingenuity, had been mostly the work of individual in-
ventors; that vein had been worked out by the late 19th century, and the nation's planners were slow to recognize that it
had to be replaced by collective work on basic science done in
specialized laboratories. Particularly by contrast with the
German universities, Oxford and Cambridge displayed a disinterest in science for which provincial and Scottish schools
only partially atoned. And it is probably not absurd to see the
standing predominance of the classical curriculum as an
expression of social values archaic in a technological world.

ULTIMA RATIO REGUM

Looking more narrowly at England's military defences, we
note signs of mental stagnation and backwardness in the ser-

---

*Still, when we calculate what the American government has done lately
to modernize American steel production, to keep the railway system from
deteriorating, or to help the auto industry convert to production of more
salable commodities, we become aware of the immense inertias shackling
industrial change. The future is all contingency and calculation; perhaps
the only emotion that makes it real for us is blind panic.

vices themselves and in the civilian apparatus controlling them. The navy, traditionally the favored arm, was least subject to mental torpor, though there perhaps it might have been more forgivable. Wooden ships with muzzle-loading cannon had a long and glorious history, since before the days of Drake and the Armada; their advantages were impressive. With periodic care, such vessels would last for half a century and more; the cannon need not and indeed could not be made with rifling or to exact tolerances.* Because Britain had such a long head start in naval construction, her cadre of skilled shipwrights and naval designers gave her a cushion of technical skills that other nations would require decades to match.

With the coming of iron- and steel-clad battleships, all this changed radically; to its credit the service changed with a minimum of foot-dragging. Arguments over the relative merits of paddle wheels and screw propellors were not allowed to drag on; on April 3, 1845, two vessels, one of each sort, were hitched together, stern to stern, and "Rattler" towed "Alecto" backward at the rate of two and a half knots. Armor plate and explosive shells, having proved their value in Crimea and the American civil war, were adopted at once. Breech-loading cannon were a little harder to accept; they were not only more complex in themselves but required the development of new sorts of slow-burning powder (cordite) if they were not to burst under their own pressures. Slow-burning powder made possible long barrels, which extended the range of fire, and so complex mechanisms were needed for finding the range swiftly and firing the guns in quick salvos. Hardened armor plate led to the development of armor-piercing shells on the one hand, and of underwater torpedos on the other. A special ef-

---

*As late as 1883, when Captain John Fisher was appointed to the gunnery school at Portsmouth, he found only smooth-bore guns being used for instruction; as the most alert and up-to-date student of ordnance in his time, he was not slow in changing that.

fect of these rapidly accumulating changes was their impact on the budget. One ship of a new model rendered obsolete whole squadrons of older vessels; the British *Dreadnought*, of 1906, was a particularly shrewd stroke in this regard, for it imposed on Germany the necessity not only of building an equivalent ship but also of widening the Kiel canal to accommodate it. In Germany, which combined a modern, efficient steel industry with autocratic traditions, the Kaiser had no trouble in getting for "mein" Tirpitz just about everything he wanted; in England, the pain of steadily expanding budgets was acute. It was, naturally, the Germans with their smoldering sense of inferiority, who turned down all proposals for arms control or arms limitation, and in the end they came very close indeed to upsetting British superiority at sea. At the climactic battle of Jutland (May 31, 1916), the Germans had all the best of it, technologically. British losses were heavier than German losses by approximately two to one; had they not had considerable numerical superiority to start with, the British would certainly have lost the battle, and with it the war. Thus, though the British navy did better than any other service in keeping up with developments in the art (and in the end saved the nation because of it), they did so at such enormous expense that whole new classes of taxation had to be developed to keep up. Even so, in peripheral fields such as submarine warfare making use of torpedos, mine warfare, and the use of naval aviation, the Germans gained unquestioned advantage.

Shortsighted conservatism and obstinate resistance to change were much more deeply rooted in the army and, being concentrated in the upper staff, were much harder to overcome. Stubbornly opposed to change of any sort was the Duke of Cambridge, cousin to Queen Victoria and commander in chief from 1887 to 1895, a period during which he actively obstructed every reform proposal. From the abolition of flogging to the adoption of breech-loading cannon and the termination of purchase of commissions, he stood solidly against all progressive ideas. Edward Viscount Cardwell and a little group of enlightened associates proposed most of these reforms and forced some of them down the throats of the Colonel Blimps who controlled the war office, but the most important of their proposals, for the creation of a general staff, was successfully warded off—with the result that for the Boer War there never existed a concerted, coherent plan of action and the armed forces of Britain, alone among those of the European continent, entered World War I without a competent and practiced general staff.

Behind most of these instances of recalcitrance we recognize stupidity, to be sure, but also the operation of a rigid caste system that invites, as much as any piece of social paralysis, the metaphors of hardened arteries and stiffened joints. Purchase of commissions was purely and simply an issue of caste and status—those in the gentlemen's club were hostile to the bounders outside it and actually argued that men of superior competence in the army could become a threat to the social order: being good at the war business, they would seek opportunities to show off their talents. A gentlemanly amateur might be counted on to make a muddle of things; but then, knowing himself to be a muddler, he wouldn't seek opportunities to display the fact. This sort of thinking, or something like it, went beyond mere stupidity. The hardest knots of resistance to change formed around the cavalry. Cavalry regiments were the natural refuge of the horsy, fox-hunting, polo-playing set; hard to budge at any time, their minds were set in concrete by the experience of the Boer War, where in fact the nature of the terrain and the character of the opposition made mounted riflemen a decisive force. Men who did first-rate service there were promoted to staff positions with all their prejudices and prepossessions intact—and so came to command in the First World War, where, with all their irrelevant experience firmly fixed in their solid heads, they came up against barbed wire, entrenchments in depth, and enfilading machine-gun fire. Obsolete machinery is hard to deal with when an aging society wants to remain vital; obsolete human materials are infinitely harder. One striking example of handling the problem well may be noted. After the six-day war, all of Israel's lieutenant-generals were properly thanked, pensioned, and sent off to find new careers, on the wise presumption that for the next war they would be too old and inflexible. It is an ungrateful task to dismiss a successful performer at the height of his success, but in the racetrack world of modern technology, where the temptation to repeat one's established performance is always a first step backwards, it is probably a good idea for the career of a professional soldier to be as short as that of a professional athlete. There is an old and bitter saying that British generals are always perfectly prepared for the war *before* the one in which they have to fight; surely that is an avoidable error, and the more often a society repeats known and avoidable errors, the more likely it is to be labelled, and properly labelled, decadent.

In one important though indirect way, Britain had been preparing for the 1914 war in a spirit the very reverse of decadent ever since 1832. At that time, it will be recalled, the House of Lords sullenly and against its own wishes consented to passage of the Reform Bill. For forty years, propertied England had been dreading an irresistible flood of working-class demands, such as had accompanied the revolution in France. The decision of 1832 was to soften these demands by partially giving way to them, and that first decision led, as doomsayers had freely predicted in 1832 and before, to further demands and further givings-way. A political center of gravity that the first reform bill moved toward the wealthy middle class, the second reform bill of Disraeli transferred to the small owner and rate payer. Under the leadership of Mr. Gladstone and with the help of the trade union movement, substantial improvements were won in wages and hours, in unemployment insurance, in access to education, and in the beginnings of slum clearance and housing developments. Slowly the whole substructure of the welfare state fell into place, its substantial cost financed primarily by a graduated income tax. Strident propagandists might complain that these concessions of the propertied to the working classes fell short of bare justice; in isolated instances, there were strikes of great bitterness and massive protest marches. But as the twentieth century moved through its first decade and a half, it was not hard to recognize the really enraged and desperate groups of English society—and the working class was not among them.

Three uncompromised issues tore like vultures at the liver of liberal England. One was the forced self-castration of the House of Lords, which under extreme pressure voted to deny itself any significant role in the legislative process; a second was the right of women to vote; and a third was the impossibility of reconciling Home Rule for Ireland with the fanatical loyalty of Ulster to a God who was not so much Protestant or British as He was antipapist. One can see the second and third of these bitter issues as outgrowths of the first: the Tories, crudely and unfairly (as they saw it) deprived of their voice in the Lords, set their feet in concrete on the issue of suffrage and deliberately inflamed the most fanatical passions in Ulster to delay or destroy Home Rule. As it was, the bitterness of English politics in the last few years before the war persuaded the Kaiser's advisers that Albion was hopelessly divided, politically impotent, ripe for dissolution and defeat. It was a mistaken judgment, but if in 1914 the working class had been as deeply embittered as the Tories were, it might have been right.

Whether the English working class, or for that matter the German, should have supported their leaders in what was essentially an imperialist war is a question to itself; before the struggle ground to a halt, much more was involved than imperial possessions or trade monopolies. And the fact is that Englishmen fought with more spirit in the First World War, as they later fought in a better one, for the sense of an investment they had made in the society. The Beveridge Report of 1941 was so powerful a force for British morale that Hitler flatly forbade his propagandists to mention it at all. Just stay away from it was the line.

The contrast with those societies already stigmatized as decadent could hardly be more striking. The best of them, the Byzantine, did not give its lower orders even a fraction of the share in society and its future that the British did. Not only in the positive sense, by offering goodies, but also by imposing on their own propertied classes really hateful and humiliating measures, they advertised equality of sacrifice as a goal of their society. Had the Kaiser been a subtler man, he might have considered that by disciplining its *possessores*, even to desperation, a society may unite to particular effect those of whom, for the moment, it has most need—immemorial, anonymous folk, for whom the latest and best word is "grunts."

INCENTIVES: A DIGRESSION

Why men fight, nobody knows; battle is a structured situation, generally, and when one falls into it after a good deal of guidance and preparation, one would feel foolish to back out. But the issue is really incentives; that issue is with us all the time, becoming acute when self-sacrifice is demanded of us. Obviously, social engineering can do a good deal to push people toward their social duty; authoritarian societies with oppressive propaganda machinery can and do put overwhelming pressure on their subjects to behave in the approved way, up to and including self-annihilation. We in the liberal democracies tend to look down on this sort of conditioning as mechanical and rather ignoble, except perhaps in emergencies when we resort to it ourselves. But this sort of deep persuasion apart, liberal democracies, especially when their members are materially comfortable, do seem rather short of incentives. Religious justification used to be a powerful motive, but in a society that embraces many races and faiths, it makes little appeal; loot is no longer a civilized, or in most instances, a practical practice. Social rank is empty without great wealth to support it, and a society that already makes available to the clever and ambitious most of what money can buy is hardly in a position to purchase dangerous or disagreeable service. It is an unhappy general truth that positive initiatives destroy themselves; they are self-negating, in the sense that a man who has just eaten a heavy meal is no longer hungry. Negative incentives, on the other hand, are self-reinforcing; the man who is hungry or resentful today is even more so when he recalls that he was hungry or resentful yesterday and the day before. One might therefore conclude that self-satisfaction in a society is an ominous sign, restlessness a condition to be cultivated, and that the creature comforts should be held back, to serve as enticements for as long as possible. On no terms should they be dissipated in a splurge that would leave the community awash in consumer goods but with no impulse for more substantial achievement. There may be reason to think that in some planned societies of our day, something very like this thinking prevails.

Our traditional solution is found in rotation; we accept that as incentives diminish at the top of the social scale, a series of adjustments and slippages among the established will make room for aggressive competitors from below to join or displace them. Egalitarian societies don't enjoy this resource, or to the extent they do must abandon their ostensible ideals; they have to atone for it by maintaining chronic shortages and a barrage of warlike propaganda, the rhetoric of struggle.

The word and concept of rotation alike date back to the mid-seventeenth century, when James Harrington made them the keynote of his book *Oceana*; their application is universal. Empires based on conquest and occupation of land are notably stiff and lethargic in shifting social formulas to reflect vital energies. The classic instance is prerevolutionary France, where noble families refused to allow even their younger sons to be contaminated by contact with trade or industry: sinecures in the church and army were deliberately reserved for the aristocracy to prevent any such unclean contact.

The appropriate contrast is with England of the same period, where prosperous tradesmen in due course burgeoned into rich merchants with marriageable sons and daughters, who coupled with gentry and rose across the generations through the gradations to form a complex thicket of family relationships known as county society, with connections in court society, the highest society of all. Through most of the eighteenth century, the briary resilience of the English establishment contrasted with the brittle exclusiveness of the French—hence, among other consequences, the fact that the French revolution never spread to England. But the English pattern ceased to appear liberal after the French and American revolutions, after experience of the Australian and Canadian communities, which dispensed entirely with a peerage and largely with an established church. In this context, the movement to encourage emigration, which aimed to stimulate a wider cycle of rotation, may have had the effect of interrupting and diminishing such domestic rotation as was still taking place at the end of the nineteenth century. Its inadequacy in scope and pace was a matter of general comment at the time; for one thing, the established pattern of primogeniture, which worked reasonably well with landed estates, worked very poorly when the estate being transmitted was an industrial or commercial enterprise.

A last reflection on incentive in an egalitarian state is that the human heart feels about privilege as Auden says it does about love—what we want is not universal love, but to be loved alone. Privilege loses most of its savor when it isn't, in some immediate way, exclusive: the good is much better when it's denied to—or, better still, taken away from—somebody else. Perhaps the newly engineered socialist man and woman may someday be made exempt from this pattern of triangulated desire-cum-covetise; nothing suggests it has happened yet.

SIDELIGHT FROM THE ARTS

The period of England's most overt and inflammatory imperialism is also, and perhaps by no coincidence, the period of overt and inflammatory "decadence" in literature. What the connection actually was can never be more than a subject of speculation. It would be agreeable to suppose that Oscar Wilde, Aubrey Beardsley, and Algernon Charles Swinburne were reacting, like so many strips of litmus paper, to the social statistics of the age: nothing is less likely to be true. Victorian evangelicism, as a system of top-heavy repression, was bound to create its own reaction; the weight of empire may at most have augmented that reaction. Across the Channel, the example of Gautier, Baudelaire, and the *poètes maudits*, with their intoxicating freedom from middle-class morality, could hardly have failed to appeal. The revolution in poetry, begun in 1798, had begun to exhaust its own premises; Swinburne would have flagellated his own sensibilities, whether the empire (of which in his later years he was a perfervid defender) expanded or contracted. Besides, the period between 1880 and 1910, though it included the period of imperialism, included a great deal else in the way of swelling populations, legal and social reforms, widening education, astounding technical leaps. No doubt from the point of view of a Des Esseintes, these developments are just part of the pullulating, fetid growth of modern democracy—a disgusting and decadent vulgarity in itself. But this formula largely disposes of inherent connections between decadent imperialism and decadent literature. The more figures we involve—Kipling, Poe, Wagner, Zola, Maeterlinck, Moreau, Mallarmé, Pater—the less inherent the connections seem to be.

The decadence of the *Yellow Book*, in any event, hardly reflected the mood of the nation at large. The two Jubilee celebrations of 1887 and 1897 could scarcely be seen as evidence of social degeneration, while the real enthusiasm with which the empire rallied to support England during the South African war contrasted sharply with the apathy or open hostility of the rest of the world. Probably the best light in which to see the passing phase of English literary decadence is as a strain of romanticism with a long previous history, for which we refer the reader to Signor Mario Praz's classic study, *The Romantic Agony*.

No, if literary symptoms of "decadent" England are to

be sought anywhere, let it be in the pages of Thomas Hardy, with their evocation of a hard but rich peasant life long vanished, their often weary sense of the world's weight, the mindless roar and rattle of machinery in perpetual useless motion. Not that the society Hardy describes is itself decadent or that individuals in it are inferior to what they or anybody else used to be; the symptom of decadence that Hardy conveys is simply alienation, the individual's sense of being shut out of the system. Certainly this is not the only symptom of decadence, and even more certainly it is not an unequivocal symptom; for thousands of years, many thinking people have felt alienated from the society of their day, but having institutions to express that alienation, they became monks, nuns, or anchorites. Still, against the background of Victorian evangelicism, and the positive-thinking traditions of the English novel, the mood of a thoughtful and essentially conservative man like Hardy must have merited scrutiny.

It still does; and not least because of the amorphous, unfocused quality of the mood Hardy most often expresses. Even sophisticated social statistics often fail to record feelings as indefinite as irrelevance, which are easily transferred from people to institutions to cosmic forces. Such moods are always present in society and always apt to fluctuate with time and place. Cruder even than the means of identifying moods of apathy and despair are the means of dealing with them, once identified. What can one do for, or to, people who sense life as pointless, rewards as meaningless, the future as bleak and brief? Hardy's cosmic despondency is a little lightened, like that of Housman, by recollections of the sunburnt life of the fields. But that of John Davidson, author of the classic "Thirty Bob a Week," is bounded by mean streets, miserable lodgings, hopeless penury. Men felt the impersonality of the urban labyrinth more deeply when they came to it from the sheltered intimacy of rural villages; but they encountered it in a thousand forms, in the pages of De Quincey's *Opium Eater*, in *The City of Dreadful Night*, in the dark, evocative pages of Mr. Dickens. Whether any or all of this urban-nightmare material represented decadence or the material of decadence depends, among other things, on the intangible element of protest in its presentation; as a literary strategy, it's often more forceful to let the reader voice this protest for himself, rather than take it out of his mouth. So how much is nothing? Often the most.

THE TWENTIETH-CENTURY WARS

Though there are effective and ineffective ways to fight wars, there are not, properly speaking, any decadent ways. To the extent that one is fighting, one is not preparing for or acquiescing in self-destruction. It is in the period before wars, when their conditions are being determined, that decadence, if any, asserts itself. And in this respect Britain's two twentieth-century wars stand in marked contrast. For the fifty years before World War I, it is doubtful if "decadence" in a generalized sense, referring to the overall condition of society, is really a useful concept. While Germany was building her navy at breakneck speed, multiplying the size of her army at a stroke, and overwhelming her people with taxes specifically earmarked for armaments (especially notable was the million-mark capital levy of March 1913), it is clear what an empire that was decadent after the fashion of fifth-century Rome would have done—that is, nothing. It is clear as well what a hard-shell dictatorship, with a beady eye on its own military survival and nothing else, would have done—that is, suppress dissent, order general mobilization, and plan a set of preemptive strikes. And it is clearest of all that Britain followed in those last years before the war neither of these policies but an intermediate one, which rendered the navy more powerful and more accessible for war in the North Sea and the Channel and the army better prepared for mobilization as well as more numerous. (For these changes Sir John Fisher and Viscount R. B. Haldane were largely responsible.) Yet at the same time, she was laying the foundations for a system of national health care and unemployment insurance, widening the university curricula, and encouraging technical education. August 1914 found her neither totally unprepared nor totally mobilized— surely not the ideal posture, but one to which it would be hard to attach the stigma of "decadence" without implying Lacedemonian standards of military preparedness.

The Second World War found England in a distinctly worse state of preparedness than the first had done, and for this, precisely because the experience of 1914 was so available and pertinent, there was far less rational cause. Indeed, one can see something almost pathological in the reluctance of English politicians like Chamberlain and Baldwin to recognize an Axis threat and prepare for it. Nor were conservatives the only ones at fault; for years the Labor party fought against military preparedness, babbling of collective security but submitting as late as 1935 to the leadership of an avowed pacifist, George Lansbury, and objecting, even in 1939 (!) to the introduction of conscription. Conservative readiness to appease Hitler grew, no doubt, out of a desire to see Germany destroy Russia. But conservatives, no less than liberals, had every prudent reason to mistrust Hitler's ever-growing power in central Europe. If collective security was to work, how could it work without armies? If it was not to work, why not take Hitler at his word when he trumpeted his scorn and contempt for the decadent democracies? Simply on the basis of his announced programs, there was good reason to fear and mistrust Hitler; when it became known that he was outspending England on armaments by a figure of eight to one, it was deep imbecility, verging on idiocy, not to reckon narrowly the worst alternatives. While Oxford Groupers mobilized young Englishmen to swear they would never, under any circumstances, bear arms in defence of king or country, Hitler had every encouragement to talk—loudly and loosely, as usual— of the decadent, passive democracies. Behavior which so clearly fulfills provocative charges of decadence is obviously decadent *ipso facto*—as it is cowardice not to resent a provocative charge of cowardice.

Yet, as everyone knows, if Britain was decadent on August 31, 1939, she was not so on September first, nor through the first period of postwar reconstruction. No doubt the war sapped her strength terribly, as the first war had done even more markedly, but a nation in arms against an openly aggressive enemy, though she is not automatically arrayed with all the virtues, is not to be impeached of decadence unless she invites in some major way her own downfall. Even after the war, when the hour for dismembering the empire was at hand, though the obvious cause for dismemberment was physical and financial exhaustion of the mother country, one can hardly recognize anything like decadence in the actual process. The breakup of the Roman empire, 1,500 years before, had scattered wandering bands of brigands and looters wholesale across the once-civilized world. Hardly anything of the sort attended the dissolution of Britain's empire. Where the British withdrew, they left (on the whole) functioning governments and operative economies. There were voids into which other powers stepped, but little real anarchy. The communal rioting that disfigured the separation of Pakistan from India was probably the worst episode of the entire gigantic process. It was horrible, indeed; but as it grew out of religious strife that long antedated British arrival in India, and has continued in different forms and degrees since British departure, it makes little sense to pin specific blame on the Raj. To condemn the British for not preventing communal riots after their withdrawal, without giving them credit for largely preventing such riots during their presence, is not easy. Indeed, the present state of affairs on the subcontinent does not encourage one to think the peoples were well prepared for self-government; neither does it encourage one to think that better preparation forty years ago would have done much to help things now. Every pot, as the saying goes, must stand on its own bottom. The histories of these nations are now their own, though like children whimpering over the misdeeds of their parents they find it reassuring to chew the cud of past wrongs. But clearly what matters for a new nation in its newness is less where it starts from than the direction in which it chooses to move. Letting go of a colony means letting go, for better or worse. No doubt countries like Ghana and Uganda have grounds for complaint, but as much against themselves and their own as against the British. Pericles told the Athenians several millennia ago that laying an empire down could be harder than picking it up; except for the by now absolutely insoluble case of Ireland,* the British seem to have done comparatively well at this dangerous and disagreeable task. Glo-

---

*It is interesting to note that Charles Stewart Parnell, the first and greatest champion of Home Rule, had practically no idea that Ulster would represent an obstacle to Irish autonomy. On January 6, 1886, he addressed a note to Gladstone saying that "the Protestants, other than the owners of land, are not really opposed" to Home Rule. That the problem has now become immovably rigid (largely because of inflamed religious bigotry on both sides) is a very general opinion, in which everyone holding it would be delighted to be proved wrong. Parnell's judgment from Ensor, *England 1870–1914* (Oxford: Oxford University Press, 1936), p. 451, note 2; Pericles's from Thucydides.

rious deeds are not to be expected in this labor, but it can be performed more or less honorably, decently or disgracefully; recent history provides us with a wide gamut of instances.

For over the past half-century, not only Britain but France, Belgium, Portugal, Holland, Germany, and just about every European country except Russia have been separated, willy-nilly, from their colonies and possessions. Imperial holdings cannot be held; whether as a matter of sour grapes or not, there is increasing doubt whether (exceptional strategic considerations apart) they are worth holding. As the British Empire was not an empire in the Roman sense, but nonetheless included a major ingredient of colonialism, so the British surrender of what they could not hold was exceptionally easy to disguise as generosity. One can see through some of these disguises, as well as some of those imposed on the British by their clients, ex-clients, and concealed foes, without being confident of the truth. Instances are many, complications great; nowhere else in world history are things less likely to be what they seem. Still, those who most deplore the British record would deplore it even more loudly if it were less "decadent," that is, more authoritative and possessive. By and large, so far as it was possible, the British since World War II seem to have achieved a rough approximation of that situation in which Britons are neither anyone's slave, nor anyone's master.

ENGLAND TODAY

Looking simply at the modern nation shorn of her colonies, it is easy to recognize various soft and sore spots in the national life that, if they do not at the moment add up to categorical decadence, might nonetheless presage that condition in the future. Not the least of these omens, though an ambiguous one (for isn't it perhaps a paradoxical sign of health and vigor for a decadent nation to be wrapped up in its own diagnosis, avid after the medicine that will restore it to health?) is the growth of an enormous literature on the plight of modern Britain. This literature seems to come in waves. Taking his cue from Gibbon, a man named Elliot Mills wrote as early as 1905 a small *Decline and Fall of the British Empire*; three years later Arthur Balfour delivered to the young ladies of Newnham College a set of hard-headed lectures on "Decadence." They still make interesting reading. During the period between wars, when it was convenient to think France the most decadent of nations, English discussion of the subject fell off. But after the second war, a spate of somber, prophetic volumes appeared, advertising if not indeed inciting to hypochondria. *The Break Up of Britain*, *The Stagnant Society*, *The Future That Doesn't Work*, *The Suicide of a Nation*, *Is Britain Dying?*—such titles make clear that if Britain collapses in the near future, it won't be for lack of gloomy diagnosticians. Maybe because of them, though even that is doubtful, for the general triteness of the topic must by now have discouraged all but the most devoted readers.

The diagnoses of Britain's condition proposed in these various books are as numerous as the kinds of evidence on which they are based. There are those who say the new social programs installed after World War II, especially the social security and national health programs, are responsible for the melancholy economic condition in which Britain finds herself.* The featherbedding, wildcatting trade unions are held responsible. Incompetent management is at fault. Elitist education is to blame—or its contrary, universal, permissive,

---

*We must be a bit careful here, for a minority of the diagnosticians declare that Britain has no special plight of her own, that her trouble (with minor individual variations) is that of western Europe as a whole, of capitalist society in general, or of industrial societies as a class.

over-diluted education. Inequitable tax policies are the problem. Diversion of capital investment from domestic to foreign enterprise is a basic deterrent to the economy. A foreign policy too ambitious for the nation's economic strength is sapping its vitality. The whole social and political establishment must bear the weight of responsibility. And as for the fact itself of decadence, no piece of social evidence is too large or too small to be brought forward. There are statistics to demonstrate a long-term decline in Britain's economic strength and economic growth rate; there are statistics, just as impressive, to show that the main changes have taken place only in the past quarter-century. By comparison with her own past, Britain's record of growth and productivity can be shown to have declined or risen; different conclusions can be reached by comparing Britain with one group or another of her national contemporaries. There is, undeniably, a record of labor unrest, either with or against the leadership of the unions; there is also a good deal of racial tension in Britain, unsettling because it is relatively new and very blatant; political parties seem increasingly unable to take clear-cut positions or to hold the loyalty of their members while putting programs into action. The falling value of the pound is often cited as a signal of doom; its fall, however, is far from regular, and when it rises, doom (one supposes) must be postponed for a while. London's readiness to grant a measure of independence to Scotland and Wales was long and widely interpreted as a mark of social weakness; Britain was about to disintegrate entirely. But when, in March of 1979, both communities were called on to express themselves in referenda on a modest degree of autonomy, both rejected the idea, Wales decisively, Scotland rather less so. In any event, though success in the referenda would not have meant disintegration of Great Britain, failure in them seems to put off the arrival of apocalypse indefinitely.

And so it is with even smaller symptoms brought forward as evidence of social decay. The streets of London are grubbier and the newspapers sillier than they used to be; the punk-rock groups are more offensive than the Beatles. But only the world's Chicken Littles take changes of this sort as evidence that the sky is falling.

On a serious level, one can see that the sort of capitalism Britain started cultivating in the 1870s—a capitalism based less on manufacturing than on credits, investments, and insurance (all intangible as opposed to tangible products)—has left her, not uniquely among the nations, but pronouncedly, at the mercy of world conditions over which she no longer has control. It is true, partly for this reason, that her industrial plant now very much needs modernization, and that is a project for which vast quantities of new capital, as well as technical and managerial skills, will be needed. With the coming of North Sea oil, such a heroic effort is not wholly out of the question; whether it will really be made is too early to say. Meanwhile, however, Britain has largely lost the sheltered markets within the empire and latterly the commonwealth that were her resource when trade on the continent declined. If she is going to compete, it will have to be on the world market, and there it would be idle to deny that some sort of major turnaround is called for.

All the statistics seem to support both Britain's absolute inferiority to the west European average in per capita GNP and the relatively slow rate of her industrial growth. That countries like Germany and Japan should grow faster than Britain is only natural, since they started after the war from a lower base and were bound to improve more swiftly. But Britain has fallen, for example, far behind France in GNP per capita; her share of world trade has shrunk radically—taking the figure for 1935 as twenty-five, that for 1955 would have been twenty and that for 1978 less than ten. To be sure, mitigating conditions and circumstances surround these statistics. There are now more producers in aggregate for the world market (Japan, Korea, Taiwan, Hong Kong, to focus only on one part of the world); even though total production may be larger, percentage shares will naturally be smaller as the number of producers increases. Moreover, large trade figures are not an unmixed blessing. Multinational corporations find it easy, these days, to transfer their operations anywhere that labor is cheap and to keep them there only so long as it stays cheap. While such countries may rank high on the trade lists, thanks to the corporate nomads parked in their yards, the final results are not necessarily to their credit. We have seen, recently, German and Japanese automakers setting up plants in America to take advantage of cheap American labor; it gives, let's say, a different perspective.

Yet for all this, and despite the fact that Britain's position in the world feels lower than it is because of the height from which she has declined, the state of British industry, and so of the polity that it largely animates, remains parlous:

1. Whether unions or management are to blame, or neither exclusively, British labor is notably unproductive. Using identical machines, it requires twice as many British as American workers to produce the same quantity of goods. What is evident from this comparison would be just as evident from a comparison with Japanese or German workers. Spreading the work around is a cheery, matey process, in personal terms; when it results in goods too expensive to be sold, it spells a bankrupt company and unemployed workers or a nationalized company whose losses must be underwritten by those concerns which remain solvent and by their workers.

2. Government interference in the shape of repeated deflationary actions, high interest rates, credit restrictions, and

lowered investment allowances—all adding up to a set of stop-and-go policies—produced over the past twenty years first frustration, then managerial inertia so profound that it has been christened *le mal anglais*. These political steps were taken, generally, with an eye to the international scene and at the expense of the domestic economy; some of them at least may have grown out of that gnawing uncertainty on which Dean Acheson laid a gentle finger when he said, in December 1962, "Great Britain has lost an empire and has not yet found a role." The normal uncertainties of a world divided are multiplied when the leaders of a society cannot decide who they are entitled to be, and uncertainty keeps the growth rate slow, the chance-taking minimal.

3. Genteel middle-class attitudes and values have had the effect of discouraging people from undertaking productive labor. Because all factory towns used to be dismal, and some still are, getting out and staying out of them has become a major British value. Alternative activities are no longer hard to find. A huge and growing bureaucracy, especially in local government, a growing educational establishment, and a lot of jobs associated with leisure time and entertainment, restaurants, fashion, luxuries, delicacies, and amenities—these activities sop up much of the labor force that might otherwise have to work in English shops, mills, and factories. Many of these people are doubtless the sort who, fifty or a hundred years ago, might have become writers for the East India Company, provincial administrators in Southeast Asia, civil-service clerks in Burma or Baluchistan. Shorn of these opportunities now, they concentrate on the domestic civil service, teaching, and the soft or secondary functions of culture.

None of these three major problems is peculiar to Britain; none represents in and of itself a fatal condition, but, like emphysema or high blood pressure, if uncorrected for a long period of time, they are probably bad for the health. Each is connected with the others; they cannot be mustered into a straight row and solved seriatim. Any conceivable solution involves a massive moving of minds, and where, while he applies the leverage, is the mover going to stand? It is not so much that the various goals are unattainable as that they will be very hard to reach from the here and now—a vantage point from which they don't even look particularly desirable. A clean, busy, sunlit factory, humming with activity eight hours a day, five days a week, turning out neatly designed and moderately priced whatsits for distribution at a snug profit throughout the civilized world—with some handsome, low-cost cottages nearby for the workers to live in and liberal provisions for their retirement—such an arrangement would have been absolute heaven for the nineteenth-century working class. As a pioneer socialist, Robert Owen could devise nothing closer to his ultimate ideal. Yet for the twentieth-century Englishman, it does not look very good, even as a dream; and in Scandinavia, where in good part it is an actuality, one hears rumblings that the real thing feels rather like a nightmare.

Erosion of incentives is the problem; we are not given, we never will be given, bright new people with pristine sensibilities. It is an age of heightened expectations, when more people than ever before expect to be creative, excited, delighted, ecstatic for more of the time. Reality, especially as it is organized in the great collective structures necessary to deal with millions of human entities (each of whom claims to be an individual!) grants this sort of experience only rarely and to few. Under the circumstances, making "honest work" the sort of glamorous and redeeming experience that it was for Horatio Alger, Jr., is out of the question. On the other hand, it is by no means impossible to make work more rewarding, less dreary and mechanical than it has traditionally been, and nations where it is in ill repute could very well invest an extra measure of their intelligence in devising schemes to this end. Staggering work hours and varying work loads are just preliminary stages of the process; involving workers in the planning and directional phases of the operation is another stage. Tax incentives and profit-sharing plans could be used. Small, new industries generally have a faster growth rate (presuming they grow at all—they may quietly wilt and die) than larger and longer-established ones; the individual's personal contribution is more likely to be recognized there. Quite possibly the money that Britain spends propping up old industries could be better spent encouraging new ones. Politically it would be difficult, and the first steps would likely have to be gradual, but doing something is always better than doing nothing.

Where are these new businesses to come from? Obviously, from new people with new ideas. The competition should not be fierce. It is widely remarked that, as a class, English managers are much worse educated than their counterparts in other industrial countries. The problem does not seem to lie in the educational system itself. Many extremely clever and admirably trained university graduates emigrate; others become teachers; still others go into scientific journalism. Each of these alternatives is perfectly acceptable, indeed admirable, but each subtracts from the flow of bright young people entering management or starting new companies on the basis of ideas of their own. One wouldn't want to propose the United States as a model for anyone, but it is apparent to the shallowest observer that the countryside, of the east and west coasts particularly, is alive with little corporations working on electronic devices, lasers, or pharmaceuticals, or in other high-technology areas. The PhD from M.I.T. or Cal. Tech. who is president of his own corporation is no unusual figure; sales and production are as much his business as log-arithms and exponentials. Conceivably, more businesses of this order would help erase from British minds the image of dark Satanic mills and so diminish the attractions of genteel administration, the comforts of being part of that flexible, negative network which cushions change and directs other people's initiatives from Whitehall.

Indeed, one of the more insidious and long-lasting con-sequences of imperialism may turn out to be this British fond-ness for administrative authority. For generations and indeed for centuries the colonies provided an outlet for the improv-ing, uplifting, evangelical energies of the middle classes. In India, Africa, the Americas, and Australasia the British civil servant brought his version of light, his vision of order, to the "lesser breeds." Occasionally, it was good and useful work; always it was gratifying; no doubt it was partly responsible for that magisterial and upper-echelon atmosphere that lingers about British civil servants—as well as for that sense of riding herd on other people's ideas that is characteristic of bureau-cracies. Muffling change is their traditional business, making it so gradual as to be imperceptible. Generating ideas or even encouraging their generation is no part of the bureaucrat's task; his concern is to control energy, as librarians consider it their function to keep all the books lined up on the shelf. Whether a Tory or a Labor government holds office at the moment doesn't appear to matter much; as in the United States, both parties decry bureaucracy and do nothing to abolish it except create more bureaucracies. In Britain the problem is very painful, because the limitations of Britain's civil service are mostly inherent in its very excellence. A brutal or stupid bureaucracy is easy to oppose, but an intelligent, flexible one imposes its values more pervasively. Urbane, skeptical, and conservative, it limits, criticizes, inhibits, tolerates—it cannot inspire much of anything and has a built-in animus against the unproven. What is called for in modern Britain, as many people have argued, is a sort of economic inventiveness and chance-taking. Mrs. Thatcher's Tory government has talked up economic renewal, as did other governments before; but the vested interests to be disturbed or uprooted are many and powerful, the original diagnosis of too few producers working too inefficiently remains unchanged, for all the outside world can see.

The cultural life of modern Britain—its ballets, books, symphonies, galleries, and theaters—are features of life that nobody can wish away, any more than one could conceivably wish away the social security system or the national health service. Still, some of these fine things are the flower on the plant, and we all know what happens when leaves, stalks, and flowers outgrow the root system supporting them. To the extent that has happened and no practical steps are being taken to redress a balance that everyone admits to be indispensable, one really could say that modern Britain is approaching in some important ways a state of decadence.

One basic circumstance, to be sure, should give us caution: the problem is very recent. Measured by the time scale of other communities in decline, Britain started addressing her fundamental problems fewer than thirty years ago. The balance of trade was negative throughout the entire nineteenth century; that looks like a long-standing problem, but the deficit was made up by "invisible" exports, which enabled England to survive the devastation of her agriculture by American imports during the 1870s, enabled her to withstand German trade competition at the same time, enabled her to fight two world wars. The new age and its new problems began

Decadent Societies

with the loss of the colonies and the end of a brief postwar reconstruction boom, about 1955. Really decadent societies display their condition, not in short-term ups and downs, but in prolonged and paralyzing depressions. Until recently, one might recall, the best example of a decadent country in western Europe was France. This was not simply the view of France's critics; traumatized by 1870 and the Commune, the French themselves accepted for decades the stereotype that they were decadent. An embarrassing contretemps occurred in 1898 when Lord Salisbury in a public speech referred without specification to "dying nations" in the modern world. Most likely he was thinking of Turkey and China, but all Europe assumed he had France in mind, and the French government protested vigorously.* Explanations could only make matters worse. During the twenties, it was enough to point to Proust, Gide, and the the declining French birthrate to make an argument for French decadence; General DeGaulle in a mood of uncharacteristic despondency pointed to the seventy-two varieties of French cheese as evidence of a degraded, sybaritic nation. In recent years the French have been driven out of Indo-China (Dien Bien Phu, 1954) and Algeria (1962). They have suffered, like other nations, from the fashionable flood of separatist movements in "Occitania," the Basque lands, and Brittany. The student riots of May 1968 fooled many acute observers into thinking civilization itself was in a state of acute crisis; certainly the street violence at that time reached a pitch that few other modern countries have experienced. Even after that bubble burst (for reasons not even to be guessed at without careful analysis), France has continued to be plagued by urban guerrillas and terrorist organizations—less than Italy and Germany, no doubt, but far

*Ensor, *England 1870–1914*, p. 269.

more distressingly than England.*Her bureaucracy is even more elitist and limited in its outlook than that of Great Britain, because it is tied more closely to the *grandes écoles* of technology and administration; it has been subject to heavy criticism on this score, but no very effective or visible reform. Even France's much-vaunted cultural superiority seems to have evaporated. Not all the quibbling and squabbling published in *Tel Quel* can disguise the fact that modern France has produced no major novelist, no readable poet, no painter (unless one happens to have a *faible* for Dubuffet) worthy of her past.

Yet, for no well-publicized or tangible reasons, France is today accepted as one of the most thriving, stable, and independent nations in Europe. Those who pronounce Britain's doom with most gloomy relish rarely fail to contrast her supine with France's erect posture. The statistics bear them out. No doubt the economists and political scientists will in due course explain what it is that has happened in France over the past ten or fifteen years, and why it happened. Meanwhile, this example of a striking turnaround in the affairs of a nation which once seemed to be tottering on the verge of the abyss should make us wary of pronouncing too hastily or absolutely on Britain.

---

*A recent revival of IRA bombings in London threatens to make this sentence, written during a lull, sound obsolete. But the IRA bombings protest only a single issue; they do not imply, as did the work of the Baader-Meinhof crowd or the Brigate Rosse, a state of war with society as a whole. The appropriate analogy is with Puerto Rican independence bombings in the United States; the real cause of complaint is the state of public opinion somewhere else.

The Present Instance

Already common sense must have supplied a good many answers to the question of whether modern America resembles the decadent societies of the past. At the risk of laboring the obvious, some of them may be briefly summarized:

We are not like Rome (limiting that word for the moment to the Empire of the West) in that we are not militarily weak; we have not surrendered our weapons to unassimilated bands of foreigners, avid for our possessions. Barring massive mental aberration on the part of our government, we are unlikely to do so. We are not dependent for our supply of food on imports controlled by groups of barbarians whom we are powerless to remove. We do not have a stagnant technology; we do not have a farm system absorbing up to 90 percent of the population and holding them to hard labor on terms equivalent to slavery. We do not have a grossly oppressive tax system. (It is obviously crowded with anomalies and loopholes; there is nothing fair about it, if anybody can define what "fair"means. But oppressive in the sense of crowding all the taxation on the very poor and assigning none to the well-to-do or rich, that it certainly is not.) We have not (more through good luck, sometimes, than good management) conquered large land masses containing restless and resentful populations; we do not have long and tedious supply lines to crucial frontiers. We have lost no major wars; we are not likely to be visited by plagues or massive epidemics. Our population is large and growing larger, but not by conquest. We do not depend on slaves for our daily comforts or on foreign mercenaries for our defence. We do not have a privileged, hereditary aristocracy; we do not have an official and inordinately wealthy priesthood. Probably it is true that the gap between the very rich and the very poor is greater now than it used to be a hundred years ago and also that the chances of rising in the society through rotation are less. But it is not, it never set out to be, an egalitarian society; the most it proposed (and that ideal alone distinguishes it sharply from ancient Rome) was equality of opportunity.* If opportunity itself is shrinking, as some say, that is a serious problem for the nation, but certainly the shrinkage is not yet so great as to justify the word "decadence." By comparison with any of the decadent or so-called decadent societies we have described, modern America with its free public education, its scholarships, its minority programs, its public-assistance machinery, is an incredibly open society. It is open, too, when compared with other societies of the modern world. Some people who were born here don't like it and leave as they are free to do; a far greater number—boat people from Viet Nam, wetbacks from Mexico, *gusanos* (so-called but by no means wormlike) from Cuba,

---

*Professionally qualified and apparently respectable social scientists have been known to slip without a tremor from "inequality" to "inequity" as if the two words were synonymous. If A works twice as hard as B, it is of course an inequity if there *isn't* some form of inequality. See L. Rainwater, ed., *Social Problems and Public Policy: Inequality and Justice* (Hawthorne, N.Y.: Aldine, 1974).

dancers, musicians, and novelists from Russia, to specify no others—are desperate to get in. Most of them are ready to start at the bottom and work up; they never doubt that this is possible, and for many of them it really is. In these respects and many others, we are not like ancient Rome; nor are we much like the other hard-shell autocratic societies that cracked so dramatically and fell apart.

The old regime of France, the autocracy of Russia—it needs no elaborate argument to demonstrate their insensitivity to the demands of the people, their utter fiscal incompetence, their antipathy to commercial development, their repeated military failures—remote in the case of France, immediate in that of Russia. Both were technically backward in agriculture, the work in which an overwhelming majority of their people were employed. Until Stolypin's kulaks were created (as if to show, at the very last minute, the possibility of workable reform), both societies harnessed the most vigorous of their peasants to the leaden, heartbreaking pledge of an antiquated and oppressive system. Both ruling classes despised their fellow citizens of the lower orders as animals of another species entirely. (Russian generals used to be fond of bragging about the punishment their soldiers could endure: "It's not enough to kill the Russian soldier, you've got to knock him down." Obviously, with such splendid cannon fodder at their disposal, Russian generals had no need to think.) Both societies were caste-conscious and stiffly resistant to any sort of upward movement by individuals of lower status.

We are not obtuse to our problems, as these autocratic regimes were. They stifled even such modest criticism as was implied in trying to improve things; for better or worse, in modern America we let it all hang out. Not every idea that is expressed gets noticed, but a lot more get expressed than are worth noticing; and on the whole, letting them all get expressed turns out to be a reasonable way of sorting out the sensible from the quacky. In Russia, the Czarist government by its idiot combination of violent repression and black deceit did everything possible to reinforce the contention of the revolutionaries that the old regime was utterly corrupt. In America, by guarding the rights of the radicals, we make evident how much less liberty there is in lands where they prevail. And by continuing to reform our own society through legal and political procedures, we leave the revolutionary ideologists isolated, rootless, and very few indeed. On one occasion, recently, there was a strike at the Lockheed plant in Burbank, and the Marxist parties of Los Angeles demonstrated vigorously on some of the college campuses around town. Why didn't they go over to Burbank, where the strike was taking place, and demonstrate there? They were afraid to; the aircraft workers included some tough working-class characters, who would very likely have resorted to the dialectic of fist and foot. The academic isolation of the revolutionary movement could not have been made more patent.

Among other reasons, revolution came to France and Russia because the living standard of the working classes was terribly low—low in itself, lower still when contrasted with the opulence of the gentry. Neither society had a middle class to speak of; shoeless, ragged, drunken poverty contrasted with elegance, cushioned in carriages and castles. What could be more striking than the contrast with the broadly based American middle classes, enjoying in their various degrees and modalities one of the highest and most widely shared standards of living in the world? What is loosely called prosperity extends far down the social scale, to factory workers who own their own house, their own car, their several TV sets, and who would never dream of calling themselves *proletarians*. Success of this sort obviously engenders a special bitterness in those who don't share it; having given them, it says, an equal opportunity, the free-enterprise society tends to wash its hands of them. Sink or swim, Bowery bum or admired pillar, the individual makes himself, and it's all his making. The responsibilities of solitude often hang heavy on the American.

Yet such is the variety of a big and bubbling society, so many are the compensations to be had here for disappointments there, that in normal times we jog along, ignoring more or less the misery of society's bottom millions, on the score that nothing in life is perfect, that they had equal opportunity or as near to it as we could give them, and that if a couple of hundred million are more or less content with things, that is about all one can ask for. There are two ways to judge this attitude: morally, it is disgusting, historically, it is rather sensible, and I suppose in different proportions most of us share both of these attitudes. Still, decadence seems to me much more a social condition than a moral one, and a society that satisfies a good proportion of its members most of the time is to that extent doing what societies ought to do. Unless it goes out of its way to leave itself weak before its known enemies, it is probably not decadent. One may or may not feel enthusiasm for the American government of the moment, but the sort of root-and-branch sentiment that wants to smash the whole social order in order to replace it with something brand new—that sort of deep hostility I do not recognize as widespread in modern America. If there were none of it at all, one might suspect fear or repression; but, as what one could call a mere localized infection, it testifies after its fashion to the strength of the organism as a whole. Taking all these gross and sweeping comparisons into account, it is hard to see how one can avoid the conclusion—provisional and temporary though it may be—that America is not now to be classed with the crudest sort of decadent societies. (I am not talking about the day after tomorrow or about subtler forms of incipient decadence.)

By the by, in getting rid of gross comparisons with autocratic societies that went poof, we've also got rid of a lot of rhetorical hot air. Gluttons who eat enormous meals are like decadent Romans, but they are also like rich Victorian businessmen, like merchant princes of the Renaissance, and for that matter like St. Thomas Aquinas. Societies do not collapse at the dining table, or for that matter in the bedroom. The French aristocrats were promiscuous as rabbits, but that was not the reason for the revolution; the fact that the Russian autocracy collapsed in 1917 has no bearing whatever on the ability of parliamentary democracies to survive in the 1980s. Like a lot of general words carrying negative connotations, "decadent" tends to pick up new meanings like lint, as people take advantage of its ill odor to label some new vice by which, for the moment, they're exercised, or some antagonist they want to blacken.

TECHNOLOGY

But that by no means settles the matter. Because America is a flexible, commercial financial power, whose strength is not expressed in military occupations and imperial domination of subject peoples, the subtler and more interesting comparisons are with Byzantium and Britain. The kind of hegemony they created is, with obvious discounts for differences of time and circumstance, the kind to which the United States of America have, after a fashion and not altogether eagerly, succeeded. The skill with which these previous empires were able to manipulate depleted resources, their effectiveness in holding the social order together, no less than the pressures that brought down the one and radically reduced the authority of the other, make them of particular interest to an America not very far advanced into the third century of its political existence.

For even if we could find no symptoms of outright, achieved decadence in modern America, the signs of a mature society are everywhere around us. We are not expanding physically; it is something like a century since we made our last significant acquisition of territory outside the continental forty-eight states.* The great American inventions—airplane, automobile, atomic energy—have been adapted and exploited, sometimes to the detriment of our own enterprises, elsewhere. Gadget-wise, we have overwhelmed ourselves; we have more telephones, televisions, electric knives, can openers, food processors, convection ovens, coffee urns, and cheese slicers than we can comprehend. We have more leisure than many of us know what to do with, and so much food that the diet industry has swollen to grotesque proportions. Wherever we go throughout the land, signs of a mature society are visible in the decayed districts of our cities, in piles of industrial waste, worked-out mines, cut timberland, abandoned railway lines. We are, on average, an older society than we used to be; the troubles of the social security system suggest that it has more recipients than anticipated, as well as fewer contribu-

*Hawaii and Alaska, two recent states, both had been possessions for many years, Alaska since 1867 and Hawaii since 1898. Puerto Rico has been an ambiguous possession since 1898 (it may at any time apply for statehood, opt for independence, or continue as a commonwealth); the Virgin Islands were purchased in 1917 from the Danes; the Marianas and a few other small Pacific islands fell to us after World War II. Since we are repeatedly accused of aggressive, imperialist designs, it might be useful for some official figure to contrast, if possible, the amount of of foreign soil seized by the United States during the twentieth century with the amount seized and incorporated, often despite violent protests of the inhabitants, by the other superpower.

tors. Because an unprecedented number of our people now live in cities or suburbs, the old rural virtues, so easy to idealize, have lost currency. The old sturdy yeoman, laborious, thrifty, and strict of morals, is less in our thoughts, and with less reverence; he is not a patriarch, he is an anachronism.

I have deliberately run together many symptoms of change, some suggestive of a major downturn in society, others simply instances of the change that is always taking place everywhere, but at a particularly fast clip in industrial societies. They are constantly changing from one mode of production to another. There are places in New England where a short stroll down a country lane will reveal four or five levels of civilization piled carelessly beside or atop one another, awaiting a new Schliemann to dig them out. It is the immemorial habit of the race to build and destroy, to build while destroying, to destroy in order to build. Lowell's decadence is Charlotte's rebirth; from the corruption of Brockport, Massachusetts, rises the butterfly of Rockford, Michigan.

Life in a technological society is, therefore, life on a bicycle; the rule is, keep going or fall over. American automobile factories that refuse or neglect to install robot welders are quickly undersold and outproduced by Japanese factories which do install them. The American firms are then forced into making the big investment at a time when their competitive situation is desperate. "The present" for any developed industrial society is at least five years down the road; as with driving a high-speed car, what you can see near at hand, it's already too late to do anything about. Thus the stubborn reluctance of British trade unions to admit labor-saving devices is of the very worst augury for their society; so are incipient signs of the same semi-Luddite attitude in this country. It is a fear attitude, yet one cannot pooh-pooh it. Nobody can do anything to allay it except management, yet there are fears, and legitimate fears, that not even management can completely allay. Losing one's job in a vast mechanical society like ours is a nightmare experience; it grinds one down, it eats one out, it blackens the whole future with helplessness. Perhaps the lurches and jolts of an unevenly developing international technology can be cushioned, if not resisted, but hardly by the individual caught up in it. With this in mind, we might look with new respect on the Japanese system of labor-tenure, which seems to have the extra advantage of heightening incentives rather than sapping them.

Still, such arrangements are only for those already in the system, not for the unskilled of our own community or those regions of the world where, for one reason or another, the skills do not develop, have not developed, seem incapable of developing. Indeed, it is more than skills that are at issue; technology demands an attitude, a whole conception of time, that may be alien to a culture. One of the great unsettling paradoxes of modern society is that technical monopolies cannot be kept, yet technical skills cannot be distributed or shared. As no age should know better than our own, even complex technical data leak out through the most elaborate barriers, despite the most severe penalties. Of all advantages, the sort that one nation gets over another from priority in a technical process is the most evanescent, provided both are technically minded. For it is by no means universal that everything gets diffused everywhere at once. Some general cause must account for the fact that a few nations have become technically advanced, while the greater number have not. (One symptom of a lagging nation is an assembly plant for putting together components designed and manufactured somewhere else. South America is full of them, and that example is a reason for being less than overjoyed at the Volkswagen and Datsun plants already operating or in prospect for the United

States—such assembly plants cast us in the infantile role of kids with a Tinker Toy set and a plan to follow.) Unequal distribution of technology is one of the great destabilizing forces in the modern world; its effects are multiplied by the fact that the nations with the high technology are not always those with the raw materials that high technology requires. Even as the great technological powers struggle more fiercely for the available fuel and raw materials against the increasingly organized resistance of the "Third World," the gap widens between technical and nontechnical nations. The peon who scratches land with a wooden plow to produce a few dozen runty potatoes and scraggy beans is in competition, whether he knows it or not, with giant combines and synthetic plants that could outproduce and undersell him into extinction if it were worth their while. He exists on sufferance; his society depends, for movement, for communication, for credit, for its basic machinery, on the availability of technology somewhere. Bad as things are in the underdeveloped countries, they would be even worse if technology did not continue to be available in some measure to sustain the populations that technology originally built.

The connection between a machine economy and a mushrooming population has long been noticed, never very convincingly explained. Without benefit of improved living conditions, an augmented food supply, or antiseptic procedures, the population of England leaped forward in the last half of the eighteenth century, just as the machine age was getting under way; the novels of Zola depict the same process taking place a little later in France. Elementary ideas of sanitation do undoubtedly cut down on the once terrifying rate of infant mortality, as the availability of birth-control devices cuts down on the number of conceptions. But neither seems an influence at all proportionate to or closely connected with the immense changes in the world's population over the past century. The greatest and most menacing increases in the number of humans clamoring for a share of the world's resources occur in areas where neither modern sanitary nor industrial processes have been applied to any great extent. And birth control seems to be most effective with the middle classes, who don't normally reproduce themselves in startling numbers.

The consequences of humanity's vast and rapidly increasing populations are many and mostly disagreeable; they interact with the problems of technology, which has an inherent tendency to substitute a single smart operator and several machines for thousands of laborious manual laborers. Societies with low-grade technologies, like India, South America, and southeast Asia, where food shortages are perennial, seem the places where there is least prospect of bringing populations under control or developing a technical plant to employ and feed them. Politically, none of these areas is anyone else's "responsibility"; the governments in power are there by virtue of the nations' peculiar institutions. But in all three, the peasant mentality, which views many children as an insurance policy against destitution in old age, has prevented birth-control programs from having any decisive effect. The other side of the equation is to increase the food supply, and here indeed China seems to have done something, within the limits of her technical capacity; to the extent that the other three areas have been faced with the same challenge, have been free from outside interference, and yet have failed to take, or even try, effective action, one can talk of modern decadence—even though what it involves is not a precipitous fall, but an abject failure to rise.

A classic example is India. The word "decadent" depends here, as much as ever, on a full context; one could certainly argue that, politically, India free and independent is less decadent than India under the thumb of the British Raj. One could also look back pretty far in history before finding a state of economic affairs from which the present morass would represent a striking decline. Still, by the general standard of modern societies, and by the testimony of her own children, India is in deplorable plight. The nation cannot feed or control its swarming populations. The technology for improving agricultural production is known in the abstract, but cannot be applied; the technique of controlling births is known, but meets with insuperable popular resistance. The basic rules of sanitation are well understood, but the traditions of the culture decree that those who perform the services of cleanliness are themselves unclean. So, rather than clean up for themselves and lose caste, the populations go filthy. Sacred cows wander the streets of India's villages—forlorn, starving beasts who are not fed or cared for, who cannot be pushed out of anyone's way or put out of their own misery, useless and expensive mouths in a country where food is perennially short. Populations of sacred rats are fed while children starve. A society swarming with superstitions and anomalies cannot help blunting the critical sense of its people; Indian education does not produce distinguished thinkers: the list of Nobel laureates from and of India is brief to the point of invisibility. Perhaps Rabindranath Tagore, though he was oriented as much to the west as the east, could count for one.

India, southeast Asia, and the Andean communities of South America provide instant refutation of those popular sentimentalities about the beauties of primitive life, the recurrent delusion that modern man can live simply without the constraints and complexities of high technology. No doubt a few scattered individuals with the high-principled stubbornness of a Thoreau may for demonstration purposes till their private bean patches while living in homemade cabins with hand-dug latrines, contaminated water supplies, and inefficient stone fireplaces (mortared with handmade cement), but not many, not for long, and not as a rule without outside help. For populations in the hundreds of millions, doing without scientific technology means death, quick or slow, on a scale no civilized country can contemplate.

Dimensions are the greater part of the problem. Energy alternatives that look simple and democratic because the materials are ready to hand (wood, wind, the sun) turn out to be feasible only for a few hardy, energetic individuals in specially favored locations. Raising your own food is fun as a part-time hobby, drudgery and something worse when it's a matter of raising and processing all your staples for every meal, 365 days a year. The multiplying populations of the world are just one new form of pressure being applied to the few really advanced technological societies. Ancient empires, smaller than modern nations and more self-centered, tended to identify the human race with their own members. "Barbarians" outside the empire were not properly people at all; the Romans, like the Greeks, had no compunction about using or destroying them like inanimate objects. Nowadays we are oppressed by the sense of immense pauperized populations because we are more conscious of them as complete people. Those crude and simple judgments that used to flow automatically from *ethos* and *ethnos*, that pure and almost beautiful selfishness which was quite natural in the Roman imperialists and just a little gross in the nineteenth-century British, would be wholly monstrous in us. Modern communications force us to worry about wars, famines, revolutions, and epidemics in remote corners of the world; without technology, we might never know about many of them, about others we might learn only too late. Even with technology we have in some measure the sort of outcast underlayer of society that proved so dangerous to Rome and France; without it, we might not have so many native barbarians, but they might well be more barbaric.

Though the economic lows and highs of the world are defined by international contrasts (from less than $100 annual per capita income for Bangladesh and a number of African countries to over $12,000 for the Swiss), high technology creates within each nation a two-layer society of skilled and well-paid managers, contrasting with relatively unskilled workers or service personnel. We see it under socialism, with its *apparatchiks*, even more strikingly than under capitalism with its postgraduate engineers and systems analysts. However intangible, the barriers are real in both societies, not to be breached without special effort. Though all careers are open to the talented, it cannot be an accident that the children of *apparatchiks* get into technical schools as children of the American bourgeoisie get into the "better" universities, disproportionately. In each country there is a sponge or cushion to soften the disparity: in America the service industries and the bureaucracy, in Russia the bureaucracy and the service industries. At different rates, by different means, and in sharply differing degrees, the products of technology are diffused through the society, and these patterns may in the long run be more important than the way they are diffused across the world. Nations rise and fall less because of their global generosity than through the support or hostility of their own people. Charity, especially on a large scale, is a relation contaminating the giver as well as the receiver.* In any event, whether

---

*Radicals are likely to attack American reformers with particular ferocity when they are successful, because they may alleviate discontent with a hated regime; grants and credits to foreign governments often acquire, on their way through the legislative process, unwelcome strings—such as that the money has to be spent on American products. Perhaps it is with

American society is or is not decadent, the determining issues
are domestic, not international. They come down to inequities
of distribution and imbalances of production, and all have
their roots in the patterns of technological growth and change.
One pattern is to exclude, the other is to grow centripetally.
Because of the first, only a few highly qualified people get to
play the exciting and ever-more complicated technological
game; outsiders tend to get pushed into subordinate and
basically unproductive roles. These constitute what Emma
Rothschild calls, rather drably, Sector I, the retail and service
industries—they could be designated, more schematically,
but more vividly, the McDonald's section of the economy. It
absorbs a great deal of labor, but most workers earn close to
the minimum wage and turnover is high. On the other hand,
in Sector II, the area of high technology (though it includes,
as we shall see, other components) the electronics industry is
experiencing a boom paralleled only by the boom in the par-
aphernalia of the biological sciences. In both these areas a
particular capacity for abstract thinking and ingenious calculation has paid off spectacularly; here technology has scored
its most spectacular advances, the value of which one wouldn't
want to underestimate. But they touch only remotely the
working lives of those in Sector I. It is true that high technology has far-reaching repercussions; the airplane industry, for
example, makes use of computers in many different ways,
banks and chain stores have mechanized many of their paperwork operations, typesetting for newspapers has been computerized, and a new class of semi-skilled employee, the key-
punch operator, has been created. Yet in many of these in-

underdeveloped nations as it is with a doctor's patients—some will get
well anyway; others will not, despite his best efforts; and there's a small
percentage where help makes a difference.

stances, the computer has simply replaced another sort of machine—the cash register, the linotype, the adding machine, the typewriter. It is to everyone's advantage to have machines that can make thousands of calculations in a billionth of a second, as it is to everyone's advantage to have complex and terribly expensive machines for diagnosing obscure ailments. And fast-food joints, like artsy boutiques and mail-order retailers of domestic whatnots, do no particular direct harm to society.

Yet these two contrasting sectors of the economy—the high-technology, capital-intensive sector, supplying and servicing machinery for processing words and symbols; and the low-technology, labor-intensive sector, supplying cheap, convenient consumer goods—coexist with three desperately sick industries at the very heart of the American economy. Railroads, coal mines, and steel mills make up a linked triad of heavy industries in deep trouble. One might want to add to them the automobile makers, but there is a reasonable chance their troubles are the result of momentary shortsightedness combined with OPEC operations over which they had no control; the auto makers may well ride out their troubles on some well-designed and reasonably priced small cars. But many of the steel mills have closed down, many of the railroad lines have been abandoned, and coal mining, despite the urgency of an oil shortage, cannot be revitalized as an industry. There is no mystery here. The steel mills are closing because of competition from Europe and Japan; the railroads are being discontinued because of competition from planes and trucks; coal, in less dramatic trouble than the other two, suffers an accumulation of disadvantages—it is dirty and dangerous to dig, cumbersome to transport, and expensive to burn cleanly. The alternatives are commonly put in the form of protection or renovation, but, as usual, there are complications and difficulties even with the basic decision. Is the steel industry being forced to face unfair competition in the form of dumping by foreign combines? If so, it might need protection, but how to protect it without protecting its inefficiencies? Railroads have protested for years against the competition of trucks rolling on publicly built highways; the bulk of their passenger traffic seems to be gone for good, but with highways deteriorating and gas supplies uncertain, their case for limited protection might seem stronger—if, to make them efficient, tremendous capital investments in rolling stock and new track-bed weren't required. Among its other disadvantages, coal mining suffers from social odium; it is supposed to be ignorant man's work, and many coal miners themselves look on it as employment of last resort for their children.

Technology could perhaps bring improvements to all of these industries, as after a fashion it has already done. Computers are used to keep track of freight cars and to control many operations of steel mills. But in general the three industries are far from the cutting edge of technological advance. They remain, as they have generally been, dirty and laborious; they involve the manipulation of tough, heavy, resistant materials, not abstract concepts. Occasionally, as it happens, they become vitally important to the life of the country; then steel, coal, and heavy transport acquire new prominence in our minds. Some cargoes are too bulky or heavy to be moved economically in planes or trucks—tanks and cannon are first instances, but the same holds true (as we have found out lately) for the annual grain crop, which, if it cannot be moved on rails, sometimes cannot be moved at all. Japanese steel, made from American scrap shipped twice across the Pacific to and from Japanese mills, still undersells American steel; had we been dependent on that source of supply just forty years ago, twentieth-century history might have read very differently. We perhaps do not need coal in a life-and-death way; though in a world where we may be suddenly short of oil and inadequately prepared to use nuclear power, it seems quixotic not to be prepared with some workable alternative. Cordwood, buffalo chips, and the rays of the now-and-then sun will hardly suffice to keep a country of 230 million people operational.

Symbol-manipulating machinery contributes greatly to the paperwork labyrinth in which modern America spends much of its life and which absorbs much of its energy; social machinery designed for titillating appetites and marketing minimal commodities on a mass scale is a lower tier of economic enterprise including some outright waste and a good deal of essentially unproductive activity. Between these two hectic and growing sectors of the economy, the traditional and perhaps necessary forms of national strength are in some danger of falling into desuetude. It would be absurd to say that in itself this represents decadence; grunt labor is no virtue in itself, and some of the changes that technology has wrought are clear improvements. For passenger travel and for mail service, airplanes in a vast country like this are clearly superior to trains. A hundred thousand Bob Cratchits sitting on stools and scribbling with goose-quills could never keep up with one medium-sized modern computer; we are lucky to have freed clerks from their old degrading tasks and can only hope they have found better ones. And yet it is possible that future historians may point at some spot in the late twentieth century as the moment when things in America began to get out of hand—spontaneous growth (they may say), which to that point had served the Americans very well, reached in several unrelated areas the stage of self-defeat, and despite extraordinary powers of self-analysis, the Americans could not or would not take action to preserve and strengthen the hard industrial core of their economy.

The Present Instance

Such dire prophecies of the little-did-they-think variety are cheap to make and (being indefinite as to time) not easy to refute. What is remarkable is that our long reliance on spontaneous, self-motivated growth has left us ill-prepared to make disagreeable choices as to the direction and content of our industrial development. Planned societies are making such choices—intelligently, economically, or otherwise—all the time. We make them ourselves in times of acute national emergency, as in a major war, and perhaps the difference between us comes down to their thinking that everyday life is a crisis. In any case, the ideal of natural, organic growth, which worked so well when we were growing, may require supplementing in the days of the republic's maturity, not to speak of its decline. Suppose it is decided that we have too many kitschy boutiques and hamburger joints, too few steel mills—who, in our society, can made such a decision, who can carry it out? These are questions without answers, and perhaps we don't need answers just yet. But if we come to grief for lack of foresight in a matter where foresight was called for in the public streets, history probably will not be kind.*

Technology is a private game; its rules often call for something to be done simply because it represents a challenging or intriguing problem. Creation of the zeppelin and the

---

*Not even a first step, but an indispensable preliminary to taking a first step in any direction, would be the reorganization and modernization of our basic statistical record keeping, as called for politely by a distinguished economist like Professor Leontief and demanded in a voice of thunder by our disintegrating infrastructure of streets, dams, bridges, pipelines, etc. Countries as diverse as Japan, Austria, and Norway apparently have available timely and complete economic information on which to base intelligent planning decisions. By comparison with these up-to-date factual surveys, the information available to American decision makers seems to have come from tea leaves and ouija boards. In an age of diminished growth and lowered expectations, national inventory is the priority requirement for national priorities.

autogiro are cases in point. Because they were technically feasible, they had to be made; that they were not economically viable came out (as with the SST, where the figures were astronomically larger) a bit later. Technocrats sometimes reject the simpler solution to a problem because it is inelegant, unimpressive, or trite; they invent a new problem because the investigator has at his disposal a technique for solving it. (This is sometimes known as looking for your wallet, not where you lost it, but under the street lamp, where the light is better.) Big hypotheses must be refined through a long series of little ones well after diminishing returns have delivered their message. On a cruder scale, the pressure to manufacture sales exerted by a high-technology plant that has to pay for itself is often overwhelmingly uneconomical; a stock example is the annual model changes imposed on automobiles, where the analogy with changing styles of dress is compelling.

Of all the ills that technology is heir to, obsolescence has probably proved the worst. Once set up and put in operation, a plant with its complex of trained workers and disciplined suppliers of subassemblies must be kept turning out the same basic product, variously garnished to give the effect of novelty. When demand dries up entirely, there is no problem; the enterprise is out of business. But, as Britain found out, it is the marginal enterprise, with just enough vitality to keep operating with the help of a few concessions here and an infusion of credit there, that provides the really tough problem. A timely American example is the Chrysler motor works. How long it should be kept going with government loans and union easements is a decision calling for quantities of detailed information. But when the supply of gasoline is painfully uncertain, the foreign competition pressing, and the demand for new automobiles greatly shrunken, it seems strangely inflexible never even to ask whether the plant cannot be converted to something more in line with current realities than extra cars. During wartime, such transitions were commonplace, and for years Chrysler was kept going largely by an infusion of government orders for tanks. But why not something else, something nonmilitary? Why not a more politely titled Office for Moribund Industries (OMI), which would think and make suggestions about such changeovers? An alert society would see the need of getting the American economy off its heavy reliance on the automobile. Failure to think about changing the priorities suggests a clumsiness of adaptation which, in the contemporary context, could be self-destructive; and deliberate self-destruction is one of our hallmarks of a decadent society.

Modern factories are commonly built with open spaces and a minimum of immovable installations, so the machines can be replaced or rearranged as required. It is a pity the same kind of free adaptability cannot be engineered into the minds of management. (They might be led, for example, to look into the psychological effects of putting the entire work force into a single enormous room—not to mention the results of continuous high noise levels.) But technology in its absorption with its own technical problems often blinds itself to considerations that one would think must be immediate and obvious. Fighter aircraft have been designed and built, so choked with electronic equipment that they had trouble getting off the ground; automatic heating systems are almost guaranteed to work only on the hottest day of the year; and kits are still on sale for converting automatic to manual transmissions in automobiles. It was an intelligent and enlightened company that after years of development produced an office machine so sensitive and complex that it reduced all its operators to hysteria and nervous breakdowns. Once on track, people are very hard to untrack, especially when what they are doing has a logic of its own. The future has no present constituency to speak for it. So major adaptive changes are thought about only a little, only intermittently, under immediate pressure from those menaced by the change. And meanwhile, as the proverb long ago declared, everybody's business continues to be nobody's business.

Society's reluctance or incapacity to think of minimal practical actions with limited ends in view contrasts interestingly with the national addiction to grandiose idealistic aspirations, expressed in increasingly meaningless slogans. Converting Chrysler to a new order of production, protecting while modernizing the steel industry, rehabilitating the essential railroads—these are what one could call manipulative problems. They call for actions that can be defined, with beginnings and ends; human beings could conceivably take them and hope to alter a definable situation. But over the past few decades the society has been deluged with proposals to eliminate poverty from the nation and hunger from the world, to protect human rights everywhere, establish new frontiers, construct great societies, and revive the spirit that made America great. All these gassy positives have naturally been accompanied by equally gassy negatives, as that the nation is suffering a spiritual malaise, that it has lost its sense of direction, its faith in the future, its moral fiber—that, in a word, it has become decadent. Very likely each of these phrases, the negative as well as the positive, points at some fragment of recognizable truth. Living in a nation founded during the century of lights and standing on a declaration of resonant, general aspirations, Americans are particularly given to pious platitudes and fall easy prey to the fallacies of symbolic action. Setting practical, provisional medium-range goals and then working steadily toward them is not a national forte. At best, democratic government does not encourage it, and under the rule of electronic media and public-opinion polls, which play to the short attention span and the gut reaction—off the top of one's head, off the tip of one's tongue—realistic social planning is actively discouraged. Perhaps sometime public debate can be carried on without the sweeping generalities, grandiloquent promises, and scare charges that are currently the stuff of popular rhetoric. Or if that is too much to hope for, reason may enter quietly by the back door after the public fireworks have fizzled out. The trouble is that other stealthy influences enter with her, and in the bump and shove of interests, it is unlikely that long-term policy will amount to much more than an accident.

Technology altogether out of intelligent control is most evident in what is called the "arms race" and particularly in failure to control proliferation of the atomic bomb. But, disagreeable as the implications of this situation are, they do not seem to have anything much to do with decadence. Any of us could be incinerated at any minute by the mere push of a distant button; the fact puts a heavy discount on traditional forms of military prowess—courage, strength, and the like. Those who must hold their fingers on the atomic trigger are tested by an extraordinary combination of boredom and anxiety; the rest of us must bed down daily with the sort of apprehension that used to be called "paranoid." No rational society can now hope to dominate the world as empires of the past used to do—by possessing a navy equal to the combined force of any two possible opponents. By making international war inconceivably terrible, the bomb has made international law more desirable but not necessarily more attainable. Values have shifted up and down the line; even when we are not conscious of it, the sense of helplessness beneath overwhelming force contributes, I am convinced, to something shrill and angry in our public life. But the bomb is also a great equalizer and pacifier. If we are going to be nuked back to the stone age, it matters very little whether we depart from a primitive or a decadent state. And if, as we are bound to think, there is going to be a future to be lived as well as we can, we had better get on with it. On an international scale, and with difficulties multiplied a thousandfold, the bomb poses that same problem of directing technology's spontaneous growth and exfoliation that we face domestically. It requires surrendering a measure of that national sovereignty we have enjoyed for so long that it strikes us as natural, inalienable; it demands that we trust what are demonstrably untrustworthy, international organizations. But the penalty for declining these challenges is not decadence, it is extinction.

On a less apocalyptic level, a paradox on technology and human life presents itself. On the one hand, by making modern war painfully expensive, technology has largely put an end to the murder-and-plunder business that occupies so much of the history of the race. Through rapes and cattle-raids, kidnappings, and plain armed robbery, the sorry story goes back to the very roots of the human enterprise. As late as the eighteenth century it was accepted practice for men to hire themselves out, or for princes to hire out their armies, to some aggressive monarch, for whom it was always easier to pay off his troops in loot than in cash. A few hired mercenaries and soldiers of fortune are still to be found, but not many, and they generally want to be paid in advance, in hard coin, and lots of it. The adventurous, lighthearted smashing-and-wrecking excursion, undertaken for thrills as much as profit, seems to be finished, and I expect the high cost of warfare, as much as anything, finished it.

Technology, on the other hand, has put deadly force in the hands of millions of individuals—unscrupulous, fanatical, or insane—whose access to it used to be more limited. The gross, inescapable example is the epidemic of handguns in America; if a society cannot control this particularly fearful form of technology run rampant, or even recognize the need to control it, there is little hope of its doing anything else. Societies more rational than our own do control their firearms and are rewarded by homicide rates only a fraction of our own. That the Japanese example, or the British, counts for nothing in American thinking—that the nation's president cannot even learn from an attack on his own life—suggests an order of obtuseness for which "decadent" is all too kind a word.

But the diffusion of deadly force through modern society goes far beyond equipping petty criminals or plain maniacs with hand-artillery. Terrorist groups throughout the world rely on killing, random or symbolic, to gain publicity for their cause; random killings are better than motivated killings because they cannot be protected against, and they diffuse terror more widely. Technology supplies the secret assassin with a rich array of deadly devices, possession of which creates a compulsion to use them almost independent of any political or social motivation. The fellow who recently came close to assassinating the pope was almost pure of any motive other than the desire to perform a notorious murder. His political views could never be made clear; his record placed him on the right, his professions on the left. He had apparently wavered as to who his victim should be—the Queen of England, the pope, or somebody else. The one sure thing was that he had to kill somebody prominent; the gun possessed him, rather than he it. Yet he was far from a lone psychotic; money, passports, guns, and concealment from the police were made freely available to him. Quite a number of somebodies clearly wanted someone murdered, and so long as the victim was well known, cared not a rap who it might be. It is an interesting revelation of submerged, incoherent rage— underground politics so choked and inarticulate that it can speak only through the mouth of a gun held by a madman.

Little as we know of the murderer and his helpers, they are clearly of the excluded—agents, therefore, of resentful energies that agglomerate with every inequity and every act of complacency that society holds before them. For many of these inequities and complacencies technology was responsible in the first place; despite every gesture, despite every intention to the contrary, what it creates is an elitist society. Then it focuses on a few individuals the spotlight of instant worldwide publicity; it flatters the forlorn and desperate with the only hope of public notice they will ever have in their lives; it fits the gun to the murderer's hand and comforts him with the thought that society is too humane to do to him what he would do to others. The real question is not *Why so many?* but *Why, under these circumstances, so few?*

Nobody supposes modern society is going to disintegrate as a result of street violence or assassinations; nobody supposes that any modern industrial nation can be exempt from the effects of industrial obsolescence; nobody can point to a society where high technology has not resulted in a two-tier system of managers and technocrats on the one hand, and on the other, workers in the relatively unproductive service, convenience, and retail-distribution trades. American society is not decadent because it confronts the common problems of the age, even though many of them are without historical precedent. Neither are we decadent because we do not insist on crossing here and now bridges that lie twenty miles down the road; all societies run to some extent on inertia, democratic societies more than most. It is our nature to be slow and unforeseeing. But in this matter of controlling technology we lie at an inherent disadvantage before the controlled economies. At the moment we show few signs of coping even with the smaller and more patent problems, none of even defining the bigger and more dangerous ones. If one were looking for symptoms of incipient American decadence, technology, with its areas of hyperactive growth on the fringe, moribund lethargy at the center, and universal resistance to intelligent direction from outside, would be a good place to apply the stethoscope.*

MORALITY AND THE MORAL

Much of the animus attaching to words like "decadent" and "degenerate"—on the part of those who toss them about as well as of those who resent them—derives from awareness of a not too deeply buried sexual innuendo. Decadent and degenerate societies are supposed to be terminal, incapable of reproducing their own numbers; ineffective sexually, they are therefore on the downgrade numerically. This in turn is attributed to a broad range of malfunctions. Either the decadents are too promiscuous, squandering in mere sensual indulgences those procreative powers that ought to be reserved for the begetting and rearing of families; or they are neurasthenic, impotent, absorbed in their own neuroses, isolated in their own psychic solitude; or else they are lost in the sterile "perversions"—homosexuality, lesbianism, fetishism, bestiality, all clearly unfruitful sexual proclivities.

This is rather a scattergun indictment, and it is likely, if these symptoms are all accepted as valid, that every society

---

*The stethoscope should be applied as well to countries besides the United States if there is to be a proper comparative measure of anyone's state of industrial health. If the figures for an honest comparison were available—that is, if the consequences of industrial espionage and theft could be screened out, if the black-market and prison-labor components were set apart, and the work of captive economies in eastern Europe were discounted—comparative figures for the US and the USSR would be well worth examining. They might help us decide which society had best title to denounce the other as "decadent"—or would some other adjective be more appropriate?

known to history will be able to display a healthy proportion of decadent individuals. Record keeping in the matter of sexual behavior has only recently been elevated to the status of a high statistical art; in most places, most of the time, it has been notably casual and unsystematic, and there are circumstances under which the very idea is preposterous. When pederasts are likely to be burnt at the stake or broken on the wheel, it is hardly surprising that few lay claim to the title. Promiscuity is defined very differently by different societies; when a man has free and legitimate access to every woman in his village, he must go far out of his way to get a reputation as a Lothario. King Solomon, one gathers, was just as promiscuous as Giacomo Casanova, though in a rather different modality. The very premises of the indictment are more than questionable. Are the begetting and rearing of a family universal and unquestionable social goods? With world overpopulation looking us in the eye, it is not easy to think so. In any event, decadence is a judgment of quality, sterility one of quantity; there is no reason to think they invariably coincide.

Evidently in the Bible Belts of America, the Victorian view that a breakdown of the sexual proprieties presages a breakdown of the social order can still be found. Since the end of the last century, it has been traditional to present New York and Chicago as the Sodom and Gomorrah of America, devoted to corrupting the moral fiber of innocent rural Americans; people who seriously expect to witness the second coming have no trouble seeing in urban decay and corruption ominous evidence of the breaking of nations. Urban sophisticates who thought this sort of thing went out with Elmer Gantry and the Scopes trial have been surprised by its revival in the propaganda of the Moral Majority and its virtuous camp followers, but some fairly clear explanations lie to hand. Television brings revivalist preaching at its most forceful and

The Present Instance

personal into the home; mechanized mailings and hard solicitation keep the money coming in. And above all the new fundamentalism taps a deep reservoir of popular emotion, the basic instinct of fear. The cumulative reasons for this fear are too trite to be more than touched on; they include the sudden shrinkage and new complexity of the world—an ultimate formless nightmare is the ICBM, but Viet Nam and OPEC (intricate, ultimately inexplicable entities) have hurt tangibly. Over recent decades, social change has been rapid, expensive, often disagreeable to rural America, yet those for whose benefit it was ostensibly instituted are the first to call it inadequate. The sequence of disappointing presidents who followed the assassinated John Kennedy did little for public confidence. And meanwhile flagrant immorality (as Main-Street America saw it) on television and in movies combined with racial unrest, galloping inflation, and violence in the streets—no wonder traditional Americans saw their country sliding into the abyss and fell back on the tightest and narrowest form of their traditional values.

Explaining the new fundamentalists does not of course explain them away; they will be a fact, and a formidable fact, in American social life for some years to come. But much of their energy seems to be going into symbolic and purely ideological causes. They may, for example, pass a law forbidding abortion in America, as their moral equivalents sixty years ago passed a law forbidding alcoholic beverages in America. If anything, a law against abortion would, in my opinion, be a worse mistake than a law against liquor. It would force wretched women to go to the illegal, often murderous, back-street abortionists, or, if they had a bit of money, to spend it going to a more civilized nation than our own. It would force many women to bear (knowing their fate in advance) hopelessly deformed and mongoloid children, whose existence would be a burden to themselves and a torment to their parents. But, apart from increasing the aggregate of human suffering, such a law would do little to change the fundamental conditions of American life. A law to compel teaching the Genesis myth alongside the evolutionary hypothesis would do a bit to increase obscurantism in America; so would a law to add Ptolemaic to Copernican teachings about the universe. They could only be actions taken in the void—and as for accomplishing anything even remotely moral, let alone socially regenerative, we had better forget it.

The value to be placed on human life is of course a real moral problem, one which presents itself to a civilized society in many forms. At life's end, must the vital spark be kept flickering—perhaps against the sufferer's will—till the last possible moment? Must every foetus be delivered and artificially maintained in existence as long as possible? Is it permissible to take one life in order to save two? Twenty? A thousand? The sacredness of life is involved in the problem of capital punishment, in the control of firearms, in the design of automobiles, and in the regulation of speed limits. The whole issue of birth control (to which the church is still unreconciled, though many Catholics have made their separate peace) raises the issue of quality versus quantity of life—a matter on which your everyday vegetable gardener might have some pertinent opinions. But the ramifications of the topic are so many and complex that most sensible people will look askance at sweeping, categorical rules of any sort. Predictably, if America is foolish enough to impose such a rule, it will be mitigated by subterfuge, hypocrisy, evasion, and disobedience, as prohibition was in its time. These are disagreeable side effects, no doubt, but hardly likely to have a direct effect on the general health or debility of the nation.

Turning, not without relief, to the post-Victorian world,

we find we are not bound to attribute cosmic effects of any sort to sexual behavior or misbehavior; the moral code has become a little more complicated and flexible than that found in Exodus XX. In fact, the definition of morality currently fashionable among the middle classes practically excludes sexual behavior from consideration altogether; we live, not only in a post-Victorian, but in an anti-Victorian world. Within some church groups, homosexuality is neither a sin nor a disease, but an alternate lifestyle, of which the minister himself may be an open exponent; promiscuity and adultery, if considered at all, are part of the process of "finding oneself"; and an abortion is as much one's own private business as a miscarriage. What, then, does the new middle-class ethos consist of? Primarily of toleration and open-mindedness, of abstention from judgment, willingness to see the other point of view—almost any other point of view. Thus it is less a creed than the absence of a creed, an iridescent spectrum of half-sympathies, which may assume an indefinite number of shadings from the feebly permissive to aggressive detestation of the illiberal. It is a texture of formulas, symbols, and sentiments, each humane in isolation, or at least opposed to the inhumane, but which, when woven together, create a clinging and highly restrictive jacket of gentility. As mutual toleration and consideration are the very flower of a democratic civilization, it may appear absurd and even hateful to suggest that they carry within them the spores of national debility. Still, I want to propose that the gathering fog bank of American middle-class niceness has in many areas a muffling and softening effect that prevents us, not only from dealing with real problems, but from recognizing their existence. The code of niceness is woven from general rules, abstractions, verbal formulas constantly refined to hairsplitting complexity; its effect is to create a downy cradle of words in which the liberal mind, narcotized by its own benevolence, rocks itself gently asleep. And this self-stupefaction, quite as much as failure to control in time our technical machine, could be a breeding ground for germs of decadence.

Do we live in a world of law? It is a crucial question, the answer to which controls a wide range of customs, attitudes, and institutions. Before public law was firmly established, men wore sidearms routinely, to defend their personal integrity. When a man inherited a piece of property, he arrived to take possession at the head of an armed gang of relatives, friends, supporters; he expected a pitched battle, and as often as not, got it. In respects like these, conditions have changed; we enjoy security of our persons and security of our possessions—don't we? Well, sort of; but if we think for a moment, it becomes clear we sort of don't, not really. There are places in our familiar cities and towns where we cannot go at certain hours of the night or day without the practical certainty of being robbed at best, perhaps attacked in addition, wounded or killed at worst. (I am not particularly a timid man, but I would not dare to revisit at any time of day the house where my family was living when I was born.) The property I keep in my house is my own by legal right—except that the law is quite unable to protect me from thieves, burglars, and vandals. (My record is modest indeed: only four burglaries in the past ten years, but if I lived in a bigger city or owned a more impressive house, or had to hire more help, the list would certainly be longer.) It is a familiar and basically a trivial story. Everybody in America knows you must avoid dark side streets in "bad" neighborhoods, take a course in self-defence, and at night walk only with a companion. At home, you must double-lock your doors and windows, hide valuables or put them in the safe-deposit box, purchase an alarm system, move to a "security" building, and/or provide yourself with a weapon.

Well, these are personal inconveniences; though they

affect some millions of individuals, they are not the sort of trouble that brings about the collapse of great nations. But the police, when they start to investigate a property crime, are now asking a question with powerful implications. If we find the criminal, they want to know, will you prosecute? Obviously, if the victim is unwilling to file a complaint, the police have no reason to look very hard for the perpetrator. Just as obviously, the reason victims are unwilling to complain is that they fear reprisals. Their fears are justified two ways: if the police find the criminal, and the victim appears in court against him, chances are good that he will be out soon and looking (either in person or through friends) for vengeance; there is also the pleasant possibility that the police, instead of looking for the criminal, will notify him over a friendly beer of the victim's attitude and leave him to his own natural devices. Anticipation of reprisals against complainant and informer both is one reason for a new and spreading program that pays cash rewards to anonymous informants. This is the rule of law, all right; but it is law eked out with a system of mercenary espionage fighting something akin to a reign of terror.

Still, we are not beyond the realm of petty crime, unless we happen to get caught in the loan-sharking business or become aware of pornography, gambling, prostitution, drug, or protection rackets in our area of the world. Respectable folk of course do their best not to become aware of these seamy underside activities in society, but when they do so, they are likely to get a hint here and there of what is commonly called the syndicate or the mob. This is a very disagreeable operation to become aware of, not only because it is run by rough and uncouth characters but also because nobody knows for sure how far it extends or how high up it goes. Since everybody denies its existence, even where its presence is blatantly obvious (as in Las Vegas, for instance), there is reason to think it must reach far and wide in the society. Notoriously it controls the leadership of some unions and the ownership of many ostensibly legitimate businesses. State governments dance to its tune—supposing one named for sure three or four, that would be solid grounds for assuming the secret complicity of ten or a dozen more. (The organization is secret by nature, conspiratorial; the penalty for betraying it is death; it is bound to be bigger and more influential than we know.) On the principle that paranoia is among the best and most realistic guides to the modern world, one is entitled to suspect that the syndicate's influence reaches into the federal government and the presidential cabinet. Why not? No other business with a fraction of the wealth and power controlled by the syndicate goes unrepresented in the councils of state. And yet the Mafia is a law to itself, following a code ruthlessly enforced, heedless of all others. It executes its victims in our streets, fights its battles through our cities, collects tribute from its multiple subsidiaries, corrupts our policemen and politicians at every level. It is outside the law, against the law, and in different ways and degrees we are forced to live under it every day of our lives.

To argue that we do not live under the rule of law in our international relations would be tedious and superfluous; nobody even pretends that we do. We have treaties and conventions of many different sorts, to which the signatories adhere as long as they see fit; meanwhile nations great and small continue to accumulate weapons in quantities far greater than they can afford for a purpose hardly anyone dares contemplate. The United Nations is a debating society, helpless to overcome the least petulance or recalcitrance by the least of its members. Failure of the US and USSR to negotiate the second strategic arms limitation treaty is the more pathetic because the treaty, the painful work of many years, contained in a positive way practically nothing. Strong nations still grab from weak ones, petty wars still flare up around the world, hijackers and terrorists move freely around the world on their grisly missions, and the open sore of Israeli-Arab relations shows no signs of healing. In relations between national governments, we are farthest of all from the rule of law.

Different levels of lawlessness imply different sorts of causation; there is an immense and fascinating field to explore here, into which we can hardly venture. But, setting causation aside for the moment, it is surely not insignificant that the penalties for all these kinds of lawlessness, if they ever existed, have been softened to the point where they are trivial, nugatory. A law is not a law unless there is a penalty for violating it; and, of course (apart from the obvious one), there are several disagreeable things about penalties. They may be applied to the wrong person—indeed, the person to whom they are applied almost always maintains a dreadful mistake has been made. As a general rule, they ignore the "deeper" reasons, whether specious or real, for illegal behavior. Perhaps you suffered rejection as an infant, but if you are caught driving drunk at ninety miles per hour on the wrong side of the road, the law doesn't, or shouldn't, care about your infantile unhappiness. Punishment may have corrective and exemplary effects; it is supposed to teach the criminal not to do that again, and to warn others against following his example. But its effects may be precisely contrary—it may harden the misbehaver in his evil ways or teach him new ones, and may make of him a role model for his peers in the business. These authentic dangers, playing on basic liberal hatred of judging or being judged, have produced what seems a first-rate crisis in the legal system.

As the problems at the base of the system are well known, one need spend less time on them. Police are often handicapped in gathering evidence against a suspect by regulations of labyrinthine complexity. Failure to observe every letter of these complicated commandments (and policemen are not commonly selected for their Talmudic legal minds) provides endless grounds for appeal. Free public defenders encourage prolongation of the appeals process, choking the courts so that cases cannot come to trial until months or years after the crime was committed. By then, memories have faded, witnesses have disappeared or have been browbeaten into silence, and plaintiffs have grown weary of the whole matter. Meanwhile the criminal, out on bail and innocent until proven guilty, has been peacefully pursuing his felonious employment.

Plea bargains are liberally available to sharp defence lawyers; they are but one of a thousand resources available to a class of virtuoso attorneys, who do nothing specifically illegal but who are known far and wide as the lawyers you resort to when you know you're guilty as hell. That is the only sort of case they take; that is the only sort of case that would exercise their talents or justify their fees. Thus a professional felon with access to such a lawyer may calculate that few of his offences will ever be traced to him, even fewer will come to trial, hardly any will result in convictions, most of those will be indefinitely appealed, and the last remainder will be shortened by quick parole. The criminal with a few connections has practically nothing to fear from the law; mobsters with thirty years of uninterrupted murder, extortion, larceny, and arson to their credit turn out to have been indicted just once for a minor offence in their youth and never brought to trial. Even the occasional novice hood who gets caught may wind up being rewarded for his misdeed with a training program and help in finding an honest job, while his victim is relegated to the trashcan reserved for crippled and unemployable paupers. The liberal ethos is cautious about passing judgments and in-

flicting penalties for which it must take direct responsibility; it worries much less about allowing conditions in which a man is crippled for life as a result of someone's alternate lifestyle.*
Because more interested in the causes of crime than its consequences, the liberal ethos tends to accept, sometimes quite explicitly, the view that for every crime society, not the criminal, is to blame. And thus, without frankly condoning crime, it takes advantage of a legal code made intricate by centuries of accumulating interpretation to condone practices that result in the condoning of crime.

Some of these ironies come to a head in disputes over capital punishment. Cold-bloodedly taking the life of a human being that one is keeping in a cage is the ultimate responsibility, and one is not surprised that the liberal ethos seeks to shirk it entirely. But keeping the habitual, compulsive murderer in jail for the rest of his life also entails responsibilities. He cannot be kept alone; neither can he be allowed to mix with the common run of criminals—forgers, unlucky holdupmen, husbands betrayed into the crime of passion. He must be put with his own case-hardened sort, the unredeemables, one or several of whom (it is statistically inevitable) will kill again—either one another, or their guards. What sort of men can be had, for a warden's salary, to watch over a colony of such criminals can be imagined; but since the prisoners are essentially wasted already, are extremely expensive at best, and have nothing to do for the rest of their lives except make trouble, sensitive and humane guards are better used where

---

*The enormous distinction between a life deliberately taken, as by legal process, and one terminated by a statistically inevitable "accident" such as an automobile crash, is part of an interesting process of psychological masking. Joseph de Maistre's famous account of the pariah executioner, loathed yet created and used by society for its own necessary ends, should be required reading for humanitarians.

there is some chance of their doing good. But of course the liberals who insist that life imprisonment must be the limit of the criminal's punishment, however many murders he commits, never have to endure the years of aggravation he can cause, and suffer.

In a Jeffersonian democracy, crime is very adequately controlled by the town constable, who supervises the local drunk, shoplifter, and sneak thief; the village atheist provides freedom of speech with its supreme test; and sharp commercial practice is represented by a grocer with his thumb on the scale. Because public opinion plays a heavy, even an oppressive role in provincial society, law and its penalties count for less. This is far from pure gain; nosy neighbors and clacking tongues rule the roost in a community where everybody knows everybody. Where there is a closer approach to religious consensus, at least in fundamentals, the church has something to say about morals; where a measure of social deference exists, custom controls many social observances without the need of law or lawyers. Law itself is less complex; a diligent, literate young fellow with a set of Blackstone and a friend in the profession can readily qualify for the bar. Communities are likely to be of a common ethnic stock (except, of course, for slaves and Indians, who tacitly don't count), and no unbridgeable gap separates rich from poor. A countryside of widely scattered farmers, each tilling his own acres, all coming together once a week on market day, needs little supervision. Life can be trusted to follow its own channels and set its own pace. Heinous crime is of course quickly taken care of; there is a gallows in the little town, and though its application is unusual, nobody has yet contemplated the thought that it is unusually cruel. Arsonists, murderers, rapists, horse thieves, and people who incite insurrection among the slaves are subject to capital punishment in Jefferson's America. That there should be little mercy for those beyond the law was, tacitly or explicitly, a reason for granting generous freedoms to those within it; and it was under these circumstances that our ideal of personal rights grew up. As an ideal, it lingers in our minds, fragrant and appealing—very much as the ideal of Frankish tribal freedom lingered in the minds of the French aristocracy, long after its social content had become something very different. They too took a very brief, ambiguous code of custom and declarative law and, drawn on by self-interest and self-admiration, spun it into a cocoon of legal formulas, within which they were crushed. In an analogous way, our own liberal society bids fair to constrict itself within its own legalistic formulas and, by fostering an antique myth, to render itself obtuse before changing and very different conditions.

The matter is not merely procedural. It is commonly accepted, and it makes sense, that one major function of a legal code is predictive; by laying out offence and consequent penalty, one enables every citizen to calculate with assurance the consequences of a particular misdeed. Trials are properly pedagogic devices, by which society dramatizes for those who are not offenders the consequence of being one. If this is so, then any legal machinery that introduces delay and uncertainty into the process diminishes that effect. Hardly anybody is impressed by a punishment that follows two or three years after the commission of a crime; by then the original misdeed is likely to be quite forgotten. Who can be awed by a legal penalty which is conditional on an appeals process that may take several more years? And when justice is made the outcome of a formalized game between antagonistic lawyers, who can doubt that very often a man is sentenced, not for the quality of his offence, but for the skills and faults of his attorney?

In all questions involving the enforcement of justice, it is impossible to overlook the curious role played by the press and other media. Run-of-the-mill cases they process routinely through the journalistic mill; on dramatic (which often means "atrocious") crimes, they focus the full glare of their attention. This, for a journalist, is human interest—that is, it's a story in human dimensions with which readers can get emotionally involved. And as the economy, or foreign affairs, are wholly incomprehensible to the mass reader or average viewer, the sensational tends to hold public attention as long as there remains a sensation to be squeezed out of it. As a result, atrocious criminals and their lawyers readily become celebrities. Books are written about them or they write books about themselves; they appear on television interviews, their deeds are converted into movies. They become, in a cliché, culture heroes; but only on the basic condition that the original crime was bizarre, sickening, attention-grabbing. For the outcast and discarded of society, their brains already teeming with fantasies of revenge and sudden glory (like the pathetic drifter who dreamed of winning the love of a movie actress by killing Ronald Reagan), the prospects of instant glory, or notoriety, or infamy (who cares?) must be irresistible. For the judgments in which journalism specializes are the strong sympathy-and-revulsion judgments. Legal technicalities cannot be grasped in the few minutes of a television coverage or presented intelligibly to a scanner of headlines. But gut reaction can. Before the jury of public opinion, the accused is never guilty or innocent—he is fascinating or he is out. More explicit directives could hardly be given. Here, by enticing the criminal, not in the usual sense by depriving him, society does in a way make itself responsible for his criminal act. By providing a motive at one end, and at the other rewarding him lavishly with publicity even as with an uncertain voice it admonishes him, society contaminates almost to the limit of its capabilities the process of justice. And for this I think it is possible to hold the new nonjudgmental liberal definition of morality in good measure responsible.

Though it has only a minor and indirect bearing on the process of social decadence, I have dwelt in the first instance on the growing softness of the American legal system, its inability or unwillingness to provide a respected system of protection for the law-abiding and of retribution for the offender. An element of low comedy lurks here: bourgeois societies are supposed to be able to protect bourgeois lives and bourgeois property, perhaps with brutal efficiency, but at any rate efficiently. The bloated capitalists and their savage Cossack minions were the daily fare of my young manhood; now it appears we've been dealing all along with Casper Milquetoast and the Keystone Kops. It is an irony, if a petty one. But when we turn to big crime, the genteel habits of toleration, consideration, sympathy with the oppressed, and trying to see the other fellow's point of view don't look so funny any more. The picture is grim. Since big crime is international big business, operating its own ships, planes, revenue-collection and enforcement agencies, manufacturing its own fake passports, holding its own trials and passing its own ruthless judgments, local law enforcement officials are practically helpless against it. Even with federal help, they are outgunned and outmanned; being ill-paid, they are sometimes easy to corrupt; being untrained and underequipped, they are often easy to outwit. Their enemies of the syndicate have a million dollars to gain for every dollar law enforcement has to spend; they skim from the casinos, collect protection from the brothels, take profit of the pushers, and cut themselves in on the loan sharks; they extort from the liquor distributors, levy tribute on the unions, and blackmail legitimate business. Having now large sums of money to invest, they have moved far beyond the hilltowns of Sicily and the slums of America, to sit in the boardrooms of major corporations and powerful banks. They are so influential that if one wanted to oppose them, one literally wouldn't know where to turn. The government, one thinks; but when the president's strongest union supporter and his close friend are publicly linked with the mob, who can trust the government? We have, one might say, a government of law and one of antilaw; but the first may be only ostensible, the second is surely the real thing.

Decrying the Mafia is a little like going on record against food poisoning; one hardly anticipates sharp outcries from many defenders. What to do about it is something else. On a preliminary level, one might say it is grotesque that law enforcement is radically limited in using wiretaps to get evidence of a domestic conspiracy so vast, so dangerous, and so flagrant. Of course it is. One might also ask that public officials do more to inform the public of the dimensions of the problem; among the public who need informing might well be numbered themselves. But in fact "doing something" about the syndicate, within the limitations of the present legal code, seems a very dubious prospect. Graft and extortion are an established American tradition, to which businessmen bow a docile neck; it is not unheard of that police in the occasional big city are themselves in on the take. The muckrakers of the 1890s, Lincoln Steffens in particular, described fragmented but effective systems of graft, which the Mafiosi during the lawless days of prohibition effectively took over and have now systematically unified. But one constant of the corruption, from the early days on, has always been the clean, the honest American businessman—easily cowed, easily led by example, receptive to the view that everybody has to make a living, nonjudgmental. These days he probably lives in the suburbs, buys his pot or a little coke from the friendly neighborhood pusher, casually notices the presence of porno magazines in the liquor store, and accepts the other operations of the syndicate as out of his reach or none of his business. His neighbor may have a piece of the action.

If it wanted to declare war on the syndicate—real, unscrupulous, kill-or-be-killed war, the kind gangs wage among themselves—government could probably do so. The various families making up the organization are well known; their contacts at home and abroad have reputations of sorts; a few courageous victims of the mob have spoken out and named names; we have had a squealer or two. An administration which saw the Mafia as a deep menace might defy legal niceties and principled protests, frankly violate the rights of a few notorious criminals, and get rid of most of them. The war need not even be particularly bloody— not, certainly, when compared with the number of lives blighted by the syndicate. Unscrupulous night-and-day exposure, investigation, and harassment, accompanied by blaring personal publicity would do most of the work. (The reign of virtue would not immediately ensue; new criminals would replace old, but the patterns could be broken, the connections disrupted. The smaller the pieces, the longer it would take to put them together. Some might be *very* small.) But of course the administration does not really see organized crime as a big menace. Verbally, yes; it is always deplored verbally; but practically, no. The syndicate is part of the pattern. It is incorporated in the common order of things. Some very nice people know people who are in it. Everybody has to make a living. Why pass judgment?

Yet in historical analogy, these people are to us what the Vandals were to ancient Rome—vampires at the jugular, a pair of giant hairy hands, throttling, throttling.

Another area of liberal aversion and uncertainty is the international. Reluctant to face painful legal decisions, or to recognize a vast and notorious criminal conspiracy in the society, the liberal ethos (on which we're gradually closing in) warmly endorses the prospect of international understanding, whether achieved through entente, détente, or a supernational organization. While liberals generally supported it, conservatives broke the back of the second strategic arms limitation treaty. Conservatives lobbied for years to get the US out of the UN; liberals have commonly been supportive. Liberals favor a smaller national budget for defence, a larger one for social programs; conservatives tend to reverse the priorities. This lineup of forces is quite natural. Authoritative conservatives put their faith in national organization, particularly the army, which liberals tend to regard as the ultimate oppressor and regimenter of the individual. War stifles the humane and sympathetic impulses of men; it is diametrically opposed to seeing things from the other fellow's point of view. No wonder liberals support any organization that promises to curb, limit, or avert war in any form. And besides, one may suspect, liberals admire international organizations, of which the UN is the current exemplar, because they are weak. A government that makes decisions only by consensus, that talks a lot and easily resigns itself to doing nothing whenever its members disagree, is the very model of a liberal government. It is an old debating point about liberals that they care less about what is done than about the procedures for doing it moderately, in due parliamentary form, after free and open debate. If a sadist wanted to cut off the fingers of my right hand one at a time, liberals would try to persuade him to cut off just the middle three and would plume themselves on a triumph if that moderate course prevailed.

On a level a little further removed from caricature, the ideal of world government is dear to the liberal mind because it represents an escape from history. The past is a dark and bloody ground that still clutches us in its tentacles; ethical resolve promises us a fresh start. The more we become aware of history, the deeper we are dragged into the pit of atavism; endless are the wrongs done by Germans to French and vice versa, by Greeks to Turks and vice versa, by Hopis to Navajos and vice versa, by the Fiorentini to the Pratesi and vice versa. "What clashes here of wills gen wonts, oystrygods gaggin fishygods ! . . . Arms apeal with larms, appalling. Killykillkilly: a toll, a toll." This is Joyce's vision of history; no man can read at all deeply in the past without admitting its force. A simple remedy is therefore to read little history and try to ignore what forces itself on one's attention. Hence the extraordinary phenomenon of a television commentator who in a minute and thirty-five seconds blithely undertook to solve the problem of northern Ireland. Hence the superficial quality of an American administration which, apart from automatic anti-Communism, seems to have no foreign policy, no sense of positive direction whatever. Behind these curious manifestations of innocence, one notes a general, almost a systematic disinterest in history. Public opinion polls are used to plot the direction of political campaigns; they register current trends, instant-by-instant reactions, and like other ephemera disappear automatically after a few days. In their haste to get out election results, the media do not even wait until the polls have closed, but announce a landslide before California and Hawaii have so much as decided which way to slide. Less open but more important is the encroachment on history in our school programs of civics, social science, government, and sociology. All these disciplines, legitimate enough in themselves, encourage the student to look at social behavior, and think of taking action about it, without the temporal perspective that is peculiar to history. Without that developmental approach, many modern sympathies and antipathies must remain forever unaccountable. The television commentator, looking blandly at the present surface of things, found so little reason for Ulster Protestants to loathe and despise Catholicism that he concluded the whole thing was an illusion—there was so little foundation for the feeling that it did not exist. This helped him immensely in solving, without a moment's hesitation, without even using a subordinate clause, a problem with roots and ramifications reaching through all recorded history.

Because of their physical isolation, Americans throughout the nineteenth and the first part of the twentieth century had little reason to know much or care deeply about the history of Europe. It was tangled, corrupt, cruel; the American myth could pass it by and return to the covenant established in Genesis I. Even as we were slaughtering off our own noble savages, by the simple expedient of converting them to imps of the devil, we were playing up ourselves as pseudonoble savages, complete with barbaric yawps. Ever since our primal innocence was tarnished by the machine age, we have been able to neglect history in favor of "current events," an almost startlingly eloquent term. Over the past fifty years, it is probable America has had only one secretary of state who could say with any confidence what passed at the Treaty of Vienna, or what policies Viscount Palmerston pursued with regard to the Risorgimento. Hard words, complicated ideas; but only through them and concepts like them does one sink those roots in the past that keep one from being at the mercy of slogans coined for momentary occasions and as promptly discarded.

"Collective security" was the code word (if anyone remembers that far back) directly after World War II. It was in the name of collective security that Americans fought in Korea, though the collectivity was only token; in the Vietnam war, collectivity hardly existed any more, security was a bad joke, and the liberals, having discovered that "collective security" meant something more than all talking at once—that it meant collective action, collective responsibility, actually doing something in a cause that was, inevitably, less than ideal—fell off the bandwagon with a thud. Collective security was dead, as a program and as a slogan. In its place, a number of halfhearted slogans have been put forward, gathering in vagueness as it became increasingly clear that nothing was going to be done to implement them. Mr. Carter's "human rights" implied an earnest, evangelical intent, yet in Iran and Nicaragua, our policy encountered movements that were popular and undemocratic at the same time. We were thus bound not to oppose and not to support them. Large strategic and, in the case of Iran, major economic interests were involved, yet in both countries America played an almost completely passive role. Numerous historical precedents suggest that a resourceful government with vital interests in an area can often, by early action, avoid getting hung up between a pair of unacceptable alternatives. Asking what we should have done in these painful dilemmas (more support for the ayatollah or the shah, more support for Somoza or the Sandinistas, words of benevolent advice to either or both) is secondary to the question of how we got into these boxes in the first place. One simple answer is that we flourished cosmic principles about without the slightest intention of taking realistic action in support of them. Another is that we did not take the small, active, practical steps available to us, which would have given us a measure of moral standing with either party or both. This need not have involved choosing sides; we should certainly have stayed out of the torture and harassment business in Iran; we should never have condoned the economic monopoly that Somoza imposed on Nicaragua. What steps we took should have been taken early, and they should have aimed consistently at avoiding the trap of two equally objectionable alternatives. They need not have been propounded as public policy; small gestures would do, not necessarily by heads of state.* The law was formulated by Machiavelli nearly five hundred years ago: in the early stages of developing trouble, problems are hard to recognize but easy to cure; in the later stages, easy to recognize but hard to cure. A supplementary rule is that in complex situations, involving many variables and unexplored complications, a single *idée fixe* is only minimally better than blank ignorance. (Or perhaps the rule should read minimally *worse*: the text of the adage is corrupt.)

Where, for instance, could one find a better laboratory than South and Central America to try out a variety of approaches to the complex difficulties of excolonial peoples? They are tormented by problems of underindustrialization, hideous sanitation practices, miserable education, primitive agricultural procedures, ballooning populations, uncontrolled urban sprawl, and brutal dictatorships, in addition to national antipathies and aspirations, and the endless, indigenous problem of orderly succession. To approach all these problems in their hundreds of local manifestations with but one idea in mind (to oppose Communists whatever they stand for, whoever their allies may be, and whatever bedfellows we have to accept in opposing them) is to neglect God-given opportunities. Hewing to a rigid line, we cut off every chance of influence—not just our influence on them, but theirs on us,

---

*History records that during the Boer War, Sir Henry Campbell-Bannerman, then in opposition, strongly protested conditions in the camps where the Boer prisoners were being kept. When he became in his turn prime minister, peace and reconciliation advanced much faster in South Africa, because of the words he had spoken five years before. Where was the American opposition party when Savak was torturing political prisoners in Iran?

as we conceivably become more aware of their aspirations and needs, in the context of their developing societies. A program of directed experiment is the diametrical opposite of a program of dogmatic ignorance. It need not be tried everywhere in the same form or all at once; it invites cooperation and guidance instead of laying down the law from Washington on high. The pure-minded will say we have no business interfering with other powers at all—for good, for evil, for their ends or ours. But this is perhaps confusing virtue with deliberate stupidity, a common North American hallucination.

In the world as it has become, a great power with liberal pretensions has a tremulously narrow and twisting path to walk; the most insidious of its difficulties are those involving the relation between words and things. Abstract and categorical rules, proclaimed as unyielding principles, may prevent an administration from recognizing developing situations. Pious phrases, being cheap, may so satisfy the national ego as to obscure the need for practical actions. The power of the press to select its perspectives and emphasize gruesome details gives it something close to veto power over any project involving pain or suffering of any sort. Finally, there is a nice-minded verbal deception which suggests that for a nation to protect its own vital interests is "taking the law into its own hands." In fact, there is no operational law on the international level—nothing, therefore, to take into one's own hands. There *should* be a law on which governments could rely. Its establishment and acceptance should be the special concern of a government like that of the United States; it should be flexible enough to allow for such rational change as the peaceful transfer of the Falkland Islands to Argentina. All sorts of agreeable things can be predicated about such a body of international law. But in fact it does not exist, and some governments are quite frank in declaring that the struggle between

classes (working-class governments and bourgeois governments, for instance) knows no truce. When they say exactly
the contrary, it is only reasonable to suppose that they are pros-
ecuting the same struggle for advantage behind new masks.
Under the circumstances, prudent folk, even though they deplore suspicion and mistrust, are bound to maintain a measure
of mental reserve. Less agreeable names are "duplicity" and
"hypocrisy." But all these names simply describe the condition of living, amphibian-fashion, in a world that pretends verbally to be a world of law and law abiders while in objective,
manipulative fact it is anything but. In such a world the disagreeable choice is often between debauching the words in
one's own mouth and being the dupe of those in the mouths of
others.

This I think is something that the liberal ethos—meaning by that phrase people committed to the rationalizing process, whether their personal political views are radical, liberal,
or conservative—finds particularly hard to accept. People
who deal in codes and formulas tend to be absorbed by them,
to accept unquestioningly their agreed-upon limitations.
That is the point of stories like Alexander and the Gordian
knot or Columbus and the egg. Accepted codes of words and
structures of relatedness are not only tools for our use but (as
we have to keep relearning) active agents of which we are the
tools. The conversion of America from an object-manipulat-
ing to a symbol-manipulating society is everywhere to be read
in the world around us. Farmers convert to bureaucrats, mechanics to real-estate salesmen or advertising executives—if
not instantly, at least from one generation to the next. It is
progress, it is rising in the world: your children go to college
so they can wear a white shirt, sit at a big desk, and make a lot
of money without getting their hands dirty. It is the bourgeois-

ification of America; we have all seen it happen. And it carries with it, both as reward and as penalty, a mixed bag of inhibitions, constraints, and timidities. Social life is infinitely gentler and smoother when we can discuss "in a civilized way" contrasting points of view, outlooks on life other than our own. Yet civilized flexibility of outlook slips easily into uncertainty and self-doubt. Our most cherished qualities of urbanity and tolerance may become our deepest sources of weakness. Sitting down to discuss common problems with a man who is your deadly enemy may easily lead to a rational analysis of your right to exist—and then, if you do not throw over the table and smash his face, you are not being polite, you are being something for which there are many uglier names.

Does America have any deadly enemies? Maybe yes, maybe no. But where the possibility exists, one form of decadence may well consist of being too nice to envisage the possibility. In the new symbol-intoxicated Brahminical caste of America—disdainful of the few constraints in the least constrained society on earth, unable even to conceive of societies based on class struggle, class dictatorship, and the systematic reign of terror—I sense a willful naiveté, a deliberate effort at a second political virginity, that even in the early stages smells rotten.

MALAISE, NARCISSISM, AND OTHER MYTHICAL BEASTS: OSSIFICATION, A REAL ONE

"Comfortable" is an interesting contemporary value-word. "I'm not comfortable with"—whatever it is, my laxative, my work, or the new national administration. It's a purely subjective judgment: not that there's anything wrong out there, just that I don't feel right about it. I haven't thought about it, or tried to discriminate; I feel bad, and that's ultimate. Recently Christopher Lasch provided us, though but briefly, with an equivalent word that combined the advantages of total vagueness with the cachet of French: *malaise*. We in America, he concluded, are decadent, in an undefined sense, because suffering from malaise, an undefined condition, the major form of which is narcissism, used in a sense peculiar to the author. It is not that we adore ourselves, but that we are self-centered, self-absorbed. Professor Lasch had discovered the "me-generation."*

To be sure, as Lasch is a historian by trade, it will not surprise him to be reminded that other generations before 1978 and societies other than the United States of America have included their share of egotists. A short course in the fiction of Balzac could serve as an introduction to the subject. Early egotists were not exactly like their modern counterparts of course; moral coloration, vicious or virtuous, was freely applied to the attitude. Much that the church preached against, under the name of pride, was self-centeredness; much that monasteries and nunneries fostered under the name of religious contemplation was essentially self-inspection, narcissism. There is no human trait that disguises itself more readily or more variously than self-fascination. Still, one major difference between Lasch and all previous critics of the attitude is that he has had access to psychoanalytic journals, as they did not. Indeed, a great part of his case, that American society is suffering from narcissism, which produces a malaise that results in decadence, depends on his study of the American psychoanalytic journals.

It is very much to be regretted that we have no equivalent journals from the different societies of our own time, or

---

The Culture of Narcissism (New York: W. W. Norton, 1978).

from other periods of history, that would help us decide how far our country is like others—give or take a bit of terminology—and how far idiosyncratic. There would be many disguises to uncover, many lines of analogy to stretch. But the peculiar character of Lasch's American evidence gives us strong reason to suspect that his results are warped, even in terms of the one society he has tried to represent.

For who are the patients who get written up in psychoanalytical journals? Not, surely, a cross section of the American populace. An unusual proportion of American analysts are to be found not very far from Park Avenue and Beverly Hills; theirs is not a random distribution through the populace, nor are their patients representative of the society. Unquestionably they are richer on average, almost certainly they are older; it is a fair guess that females outnumber males more than in society at large. Out of many patients, the few written up in the journals are those who have been able to develop novel and interesting complaints, of special interest to the psychiatric profession; they are pioneers, chosen for publication precisely because they are not run-of-the-mill sickies. Judging the psychic state of the society from a sample selected this way is like going to the wrecker's yard for evidence on the state of American automobiles. We may be a decadent society; unquestionably as a society we include some decadent individuals, in the sense that they have markedly declined in some respect from a standard to which they still hold. But one can no more draw conclusions about a society from a few individuals than about a book from a few words.

Other symptoms of decadence, specious but misleading, may be sought in the proliferation of sects or the manifestations of a counter-culture. But sects are so old a phenomenon, and so various in their social content, that they can hardly serve as premonitions of anything in particular. They may express revolutionary aspirations or nostalgia for lost innocence; they may be rackets run by unscrupulous promoters. In a nation with an established church, they are, after a fashion, heresies; in America, where we have never had an establishment, the sects themselves, especially after they have survived a few years, are close to being an orthodoxy of their own. The old analogy has it that America like Rome will fall when men despair of the secular city and start pinning their faith to the city of God; if anything, it seems more likely that the fall of the city will cause a turn to the sects, but there is not much present evidence of either event. Indeed, many American sects, including one of the most successful, the Mormons, endorse traditional American values and follow traditional American practices—to excess, if anything. They are among the most enterprise-oriented of our citizens.

The so-called counter-culture is a better place to look for disaffection with American values, which may or may not imply the onset of American decadence. Avoidance of the work-and-success syndrome is at the heart of the attitude; collective nomadism and drug-aided fantasies are secondary phenomena. For a while the politics of protest promised to be more important than they have actually proved. After peaking in the late sixties, activism succumbed to the short attention span of youth and, in movements like that to preserve the environment, melded back into the many-stranded mainstream. Had the Vietnam war dragged on, very possibly the movement against it could have festered into something dangerous to the society; but as the war itself ended ignominiously, and most of those responsible for it soon left public life, the counter-culture, to the extent it was not simply vestigial, became a picturesque modification of the mores, no more subversive than the Amish or the Holy Rollers. Some fairly staid folk even welcome it as a liberating alternative (whether taken or not) to a routine that had persisted for too long, rigid and unchallenged. Pipeline education, an absurd reduction of which was the six-year PhD program, required correction. One cannot feel altogether easy about the casualties that the student-radical movement left behind, blown minds that still litter the Telegraph Avenues of the nation, getting more pathetic as they skulk down the sidestreets of life toward middle age. But they provide slim evidence of the nation's disintegration, if only because their places in the nation's economy have already been filled by a less fractious and demanding generation. Rather, they suggest in the society a certain brutal and confident indifference. Some puritanical societies sweep up all their rejects, deviants, dropouts, and misfits, forcing them one way or another into conformity; America lets them wander around till freedom sickens them. But it is not for peripheral reasons like these that any society will be judged decadent.

In considering Rome, France, and Russia, we have pretty well disposed of the notion that the state of a nation's culture is an accurate measure of its social vitality. Modern America offers little support for any such notion, a good deal to complicate and ultimately negate it. True, the verbal arts do not seem at the moment to be enjoying a spectacularly rich harvest. After the vintage years of modernism, both poetry and fiction seem to be taking some time to regroup; and while more feverish experimentation continues in painting and music, there too no spectacular talents have imposed themselves since Picasso and Stravinsky. The phenomenon is not, however, peculiarly American; nor is it in any way remarkable that great works of art are not turned out on production-line schedules. Just conceivably, the potential of certain forms has been, for the moment, exhausted; possibly also the rise of new art forms (movies, industrial design) has taken the edge off creation in old ones. Whether the change be considered deplorable or promising, it is a fact that high culture has been made increasingly accessible to audiences numbering in the millions. Travelling art shows, barnstorming musicians, community theaters, phonograph records, and even the despised television have cooperated to make artistic culture widely available. Inevitably, this has involved a degradation; art books, however lavish and expensive, cannot possibly reproduce the exact colors of an original, and the highest fidelity of which electronics is capable cannot reproduce the electricity of a live artist in an inspired moment. Still, the democratization of the arts may have stimulating as well as vulgarizing effects; the whole experiment is too new; we cannot tell. But whatever happens, we can be pretty confident the republic will not collapse because of cultural diffusion or degradation; if Britain could survive mid-Victorianism and Russia the calculated ignobility of socialist realism, it is even arguable that strong doses of bad taste may be beneficial to a nation.

One step forward we may have taken: it is a pleasure to be rid of all those books, bastard scions of Michelet and Taine, which offered to prove that because Eliot was an Anglo-Catholic, Joyce an artist in verbal mosaic, and Picasso unconventional, Western Culture was on the skids. And while we muse over the lengths to which strong prepossessions may draw a man, let's not forget the Soviet moralists who still make it a point against the west that our cultural life is tolerant and various. No official style, no party line, no knowing at a glance (or even without it) what's right and what's wrong; people are faced with the painful necessity of deciding for themselves what they like—how decadent can you get?

Anyone who has noted the importance of tax weariness in the collapse of the Roman west and the French monarchy can hardly help wondering if current American hostility to taxation does not presage a similar fate for the nation. Of course anti-tax feeling is all a matter of degree. Never, in any society in any part or period of the world, did taxpayers welcome the man from the fisc with glad cries. But American taxes are specially irksome now because they are many, because they are collected under complicated and exasperating regulations, because evasion and avoidance are widespread, because the moneys often are used in wasteful and unwanted ways—and, above all, because big government supported by big taxes is felt to be a new and unwanted burden on a people which cherishes ideals (perhaps fantasies) of individual freedom. Taxation is a symbol of the paperwork tyranny. On the other hand, a lot of money comes back to taxpayers in the shape of services that it would be otiose to detail. (Admittedly, there is growing skepticism about some of these advantages: if schools are bad, police ineffectual, and roads deteriorating, people are bound to ask if they are worth what they cost.) Despite all their loopholes, the tax laws in the main outlines of their structure are progressive: the more you make, the more you pay. Thus they do not place the weight, at least not yet, on those who have nothing to lose by destroying the system; quite the contrary. Those who receive most direct benefits from taxation are least weary of it. You might say the tax laws in their patterning discourage initiative by making economic success look like a treadmill. But they do not stir revolt; by financing welfare systems and a bureaucracy that is itself partly a disguised welfare system, they placate it. They undermine hope without actually creating despair.

Instead of an open tax revolt, what we are actually looking at is individual acts of avoidance and evasion, each relatively small but in their totality considerable. The income tax, which is self-calculated according to regulations of arabesque intricacy, offers a free field for artful dodgers. Monitoring the millions of returns is, in this day and age, a matter for computers, and the norms for which computers are programmed can easily be calculated. So the collection process becomes a covert race between ferrets and rats, two almost equally disagreeable creatures. It is a somber, but not necessarily a disastrous scenario. American is still far behind nations like France and Italy in the unscrupulous subtlety of the public's war against the fisc. We may yet go that way; but if there is any inevitability about the development, it has not made itself apparent. Undoubtedly, taxation in today's increasingly expensive, increasingly unpredictable world calls for careful management; whatever tolerance exists for the tax system (affection is not to be looked for) has to be husbanded as a precious piece of irreplaceable capital. But such economies should not be beyond the capacity of our fiscal and persuasive machinery—unless, indeed, some blind impulse of folly involves our leaders in a conflict they could have avoided. Gross miscalculations and self-destructive policies blindly followed will no doubt sap the strongest society; where it can be exercised, we have to presume common sense. The mature society will be as moderate as it can in its tax demands; it will enforce where it must, persuade as much as possible, and distribute the nice things that tax money can buy where they will do the most good.* If it can reform obvious inequities and anomalies, it will do so; if it cannot, something very serious is wrong, and its days may be numbered. But the scenario is not automatically and inevitably doomsday.

*The two stock positions are that the poor need tax money most and that the rich are most likely to invest it where it will create new jobs. Both positions are too sweeping. Some families have been on welfare for generations without making any effort to get off; professional drifters and loafers frankly scorn the idea of a job. Such folk need help only to keep from having to help themselves. As for the rich, it's possible that a few of them, if given tax relief, will venture their money in a new enterprise, but they are just as likely to buy a mink coat or trade up to a bigger yacht. In the current cliché, both programs need a lot of fine tuning.

The Present Instance

A little closer to an unmanageable problem is the deep tendency which the tax code shares with the legal code and administrative codes everywhere to proliferate complexities. The only known cure for an overgrown bureaucracy is to appoint a committee to study it, thereby overgrowing it still further. As Death in *Paradise Lost* was the monstrous child of Sin, so in modern society litigation is the grotesque offspring of regulation. Already America is the most over-lawyered country on earth; the bar itself is heard crying out against the number of barristers. Every spring the regular army of tax consultants is augmented by files of new conscripts, fresh from basic training and ready to attack the dragon 1040. Year after year these locust swarms are at work, refining, defining, distinguishing, and adding to the volume of an already overwhelming body of rules. What the tax people say must be tested in the courts through all the variations that greed and ingenuity can devise. One cannot predict the form the final catastrophe will take, but that we are building toward some sort of systemic breakdown is apparent. A recent speech by the Chief Justice of the Supreme Court points in this direction; so do some recent decisions declaring that certain matters of litigation, involving complex technical processes and even more complex corporate financing, were beyond the comprehension of a jury and must be decided some other way.

It is no novelty to observe that litigation is taking over, in many areas, from legislation. Crusaders who have no chance of getting their views approved by a legislature may get them declared into law by the constructive extrapolation of a sympathetic judge; opponents of a particular law can shop around for a judge who will issue a restraining order. Each new interpretation of the law—sometimes deliberately made vague to leave room for expansion—opens the way for thousands of suits defining and expanding its particular meaning. For example, a Supreme Court ruling that women must receive the same pay as men for "comparable" work was greeted with delight by the legal community as providing at least a century of litigation for the profession. (This is not to deny that women have been discriminated against for years on the job market; the point is that making a deliberately vague rule to be filled in by subsequent litigation seems a cumbersome way to go about things—a deliberate incitement to that booming expansion of legal business against which the Court itself has sometimes protested.) There is no end in sight to the swelling volume of "cases." Convicted criminals who find jail disagreeable are now challenging in court the authority of the governments that put and kept them there. Having to associate with their own kind is apparently "cruel and unusual" punishment; what it would be for the rest of us to have to associate with them all, they don't say. Games are played under conditions litigated before judges, the litigation often more discussed than the game; love affairs are begun with an eye to the litigation that can be developed out of them, children sue their parents for bringing them up badly, and it's only a matter of time until parishioners sue their ministers for misreading the scriptures.

Beneath all this mass of grinding, wasteful, and often hateful litigation, one may sense massive social changes taking place in the society. Ethnic groups are altering their relation to the majority culture, women their relations to men, consumers their relation to producers, students their relation to teachers, the young their relation to the old. Both the politics and the manners of deference are in process of radical transition, and the law, with its traditional formulas of antagonism and mock combat, is a vehicle of this change. Obviously, this is not all bad; to the extent that litigation forwards useful social change, it may be evidence of a vital society. But it is often accompanied by a volume of plain, nasty quarrelsomeness and thinly disguised greed that seems to have no social point at all. People sue over the common accidents of life as if "society" (the rest of the world) had made a solemn pledge always to behave infallibly and indeed always to protect the plaintive plaintiff from the consequences of his own negligence and carelessness. By providing often extravagant recompense for torts suffered by well-publicized victims with crafty lawyers working on contingency fees, the law seems to have encouraged a certain artificial helplessness not altogether easy to distinguish from connivery.

Legislating through the law courts carries an additional disadvantage, not quite so obvious. Often the extreme case comes to court first and serves to establish precedents for cases where the issues are more evenly balanced. Legislation is supposed to be adopted after an overview of possible cases, consequences, and contingencies; that is why many voices enter into it. Quite the contrary with litigation; the lawyer represents only his client's point of view, and the judge or jury whom he succeeds in persuading may be equally obtuse to the long-term consequences of his argument. Over a period of time, rationalization and review processes will doubtless help a doctrine to congeal in rational form, but it is often a deadly slow process, which over the years is likely to leave thousands of people guessing as to what their rights are.

For reasons like these, the overlegalizing of American society, though it is by no means a fatal development—being nowhere near as one-sided as the overlegalizing of late Roman society—is one of the nastier aspects of the paperwork tyranny that seems to be advancing on us, as malignant morality advanced on mid-Victorian England. Despondent thinkers about technology are fond of saying anything that can be made is inevitably going to get used. Perhaps it is so in the realm of paperwork, record keeping, and administrative regulation as well. Our children, in that case, will have sad lives of it. Shades of the prison house!

In their exuberance over being able to put umpteen billion bits of information into a computer and get it out again at the rate of so many million bits per minute, the technologists have failed to tell us how we will cope with bits and pieces that go sour, obsolete, wrong. No doubt it is possible to erase entire tapes, perhaps even to reject information of a certain class. But how to cope with the random error here, the out-of-date figure there, when the whole library (memory bank) will have become so inconceivably vast? Who will ever be able to reject anything as irrelevant? At the moment, whatever is on electronic tape is relatively recent. It may be right or wrong, but it is more or less up to date. Twenty years from now, a large part of what is on tape will, predictably, be flat wrong or irrelevant. Of course the same process of obsolescence takes place with what one puts into the human brain—except that the brain is subject to the benevolent operation of "forgetting." It is a complex process that deserves more study than it has received. We forget a certain number of things that we ought, or think we ought, to remember; we also forget an immense number of things irrelevant to our interests or unwelcome to our purposes. Forgetting is not necessarily a conscious or directed activity; it is like a beautiful, quiet growing away from what no longer concerns us. So far, at least, office machines are incapable of it. Perhaps someone at IBM is working on the problem at this very moment: it would be interesting to know.

What was touched on here, half-seriously, as a problem connected with the automating (and therefore multiplying) of American paperwork suggests ramifications, perhaps more than appear on the surface of things. To finger them, we must turn the problem over and look at it from another angle. Two of the metaphors that recur most frequently in descriptions of decadent societies are hardening of the arteries (arteriosclerosis) and stiffening of the joints (ankylosis). Social rigidity may be to a community what these ominous, but not in themselves fatal, conditions are to a human organism. An obvious place to look for such conditions would be in the formation of social castes or rigidly defined, exclusive classes, and perhaps that is the place to start. The exclusiveness of the French aristocracy certainly contributed to their downfall; as noted above, this was less a matter of noble families persisting across the centuries than of imposing on new bourgeois recruits to the privileged classes an aristocratic mystique. Stagnation and rigidity in a society are more pervasive and subtle in their operation than simply through the dead weight of a ruling class. Cartels, combinations, union hierarchies, overelaborate or overrepressive theological or legal codes, burdens of precedent, obsolete formulae, an accumulation of cynicism and disillusion, an accumulation of lethargy and complacency, suspicion and reluctance to take chances—these are just a few of the symptoms—but they are more than symptoms, they are a very good part of the disease itself. Social rigidity need not be embodied in people or concretized in institutions; it could be, and often is, expressed in the alienation of the government from the people it ostensibly represents or serves. Rigidity is incomprehension, noncommunication; an example is when I write my congressman and get back a form letter that implies I said exactly the opposite of what I did say. One expects merely to be counted, but to be counted with the *opposition*! The message "Drop out and get lost" could hardly be clearer. Rigidity is formalized waste: an example is when a welfare program, in order to distribute a little money to the needy, must spend ten times as much on paperwork and the white-collar shufflers of paperwork, who direct and supervise the process. Rigidity is the distance between verbal codes and manipulative realities. Thinking of America in this light, one cannot help seeing ways in which the elements of decadence might be diffused through the system without being prominently concentrated in any one place—"nothing local, as one might say," but everywhere a little, with consequences to be learned from the story of the one-hoss shay.

It is true, of course, that inertia plays a part in the normal functioning of a social organism, as it does in the functioning of the human body. Life demands predictability, it demands adaptability; though not incompatible, the demands are not easy to combine. But a small, telling statistic points to the way we should err, if err we must. Over the past fifty years, American life expectancy has increased from fifty-two years to seventy-three—that is close to a forty percent increase. Though the full impact of the change has not yet been felt, it is bound to give our public thinking and behavior a new rigidity of which there are already ominous signs. The new conservatism includes some people with general philosophical positions subject to free discussion and dispute, but the one-issue politicians, whose one issue commonly reduces itself to a form of paranoia, are bringing to American political life a quality of ferocious rigidity such as we have scarcely known before. Their strength springs from the complexity of the issues our country faces, a complexity the more daunting when one contemplates expressing these issues to an electorate that now numbers in the millions and that cannot possibly understand a world strategy or a budget in twelve figures. Persuading or manipulating any significant portion of our immense population has become terribly cumbersome; ideas must be reduced to their lowest common denominator, put into a catchy, inaccurate formula, and reiterated over and over, if they are to have any impact. Still another form of rigidity, potentially the most serious of all, is a new tendency for members of ethnic groups to assume they can communicate only with members of their own group, only on "their" subjects. There is a certain amount of sexual incomprehension too—men cannot understand women, and straights cannot conceivably communicate with gays—but mostly it is ethnic. In schools, one creates courses taught by blacks for blacks only; in politics one demands a quota system for representation "by one's own people." The consequences are obvious and mostly unpleasant; when Hispanics are represented by someone "of their own," Anglo politicians will think it their business to represent only Anglos. As far as getting anything done is concerned, minorities will be in a greater, more permanent, minority than ever. And before this tendency to a growing racial exclusiveness, quite impervious to reason or sympathy, one can't possibly feel complacent.

As it is the most recent of these developing symptoms, and may well provide the most acute of contemporary problems, single-issue politics is an ominous portent. For years we have had interest groups like the tobacco lobby, the oil lobby, the labor lobby, and so forth; these were people bound together by economic interests and a degree of social community. Single-issue politics is the product of computerized lists and mass mailings; its units are people who have one abstract idea in common, to advance which they will sacrifice any other consideration whatever. The gun people and the morality people, like the prohibition people on whose crusades theirs are modelled, are able to wield influence out of all proportion to their numbers. They can do so because their positions, being simplicity itself, are easily grasped, and through mechanized mailings they can bring heavy pressure to bear on a few crucial individuals at a moment's notice. Primitive though its machinery was, the success of the prohibition party in passing the eighteenth amendment to the Constitution was exemplary here. In national elections, they never mustered more than the 271,000 popular votes their party polled in 1892, yet by a process of horse-trading, log-rolling, and high-pressure politics, they were able to maneuver their amendment through the rather complicated legislative machinery necessary for ratification. Apart from their greater technical resources, modern single-issue groups profit by the steadily lowering level of electoral participation. The fewer voters taking part in an election, the greater the influence of organized blocs, even small ones. And thus, while the central government is bound more and more tightly by directives from single-minded constituencies, overall national policy is either neglected or made subject to the secret bargains of interest groups whose "interest" is all too direct.

Because, in its present degenerate state, American puritanism tends to offer pretty simple-minded fare, it is possible that the Moral Majority and its friends will spend their energies reestablishing Sunday blue laws, regulating the female costume, and trying to define "obscenity" so that aldermen can close down X-rated movie houses. If this were the sum of their activities, they would provide little cause for alarm. But as fear is their essential motivation, they have started compiling hit lists of liberals to be driven from public life as committed agents of evil, and this, over a period of years, could have effects far beyond any positive program. One should not, to be sure, exaggerate the measure of their success in the recent (fall, 1980) elections. Many of the defeated liberals were themselves entrenched figures, burdened by unsuccessful records and devoid of intellectual freshness. By contrast, conservatism had at least the aura of novelty. Nonetheless, the omen is serious; for the mailing-list people were able to put together a powerful constituency out of at least two groups that had previously been too scattered and out of touch to act cohesively: these were rural (including small town) America and the elderly. Their notion of legislating morality, however sincere in some, and certainly ostensible in others, could easily lead them to drive diversity, flexibility, and intelligence out of American political life. That social decadence should threaten at the hands of those who want to restore moral health to America will surprise no one who recalls the old prediction that fascism would be established in America under the guise of anti-fascism.

The roots of single-issue politics lie, as already noted, in the complexity of governmental issues and the increasingly obvious inadequacy of traditional representative procedures to reach them. It is a congenital fault of participatory democracies to promise much and deliver little; when the issues must be fought out in sweeping stereotypes while the real problems remain complex and obscure, people will not be slow in grasping that the one way to make any sort of impact is to hit a few massive blows on a single simple issue. It is a sledgehammer operation applied to what used to be something like the watchmaker's art, but the circumstances giving rise to it are not at all unique to the United States. In the Orient as in Europe, national problems seem to develop independently of the electoral process and the succession of Tweedledums and Tweedledees who promise to solve them. The main point of elections is throwing out the *ins*—a task the pleasure of which is mitigated only by the necessity of replacing them with some dubious and unpromising *outs*. What things would be like in the socialist world if people could freely express their preferences, we can scarcely even surmise. But one serious advantage their system has that we cannot readily overlook: much of the freedom built into their system is at the base, where a worker through his union or factory committee or district soviet can complain about, and get some action on, the immediate conditions of his life and job. The problems at that level are not too big or complex for him to handle; as for larger matters, he is not even allowed to pretend that they aren't the exclusive business of the central committee. Democratic centralism calls for the decisions to be explained to him in close detail; as for input into making them, it is neither expected nor wanted. Quite conceivably American working-class frustrations would be fewer if the level of freedom were a little more mundane, if the quadrennial charade promised not quite so much, and the routines of daily living allowed the individual voice to be heard more distinctly on matters of individual interest. Getting heard, getting recognized, is a major part of the problem; inevitably, it is going to be easier at the local level than higher up. Precisely here, at the level of profit sharing and job designing, in the areas of fighting monotony and tapping worker creativity, the American system could do far more than it does to introduce imaginative and practical reforms. But the idea that in a popular vote held every four years, a semi-informed electorate can give intelligent direction to a national administration faced with intricate and unforeseen problems goes against all common sense. A great deal of flattery and a good deal of hypocrisy enter into the assumption that in a modern society, ostensibly democratic, the people decide anything. Likely this has been true since the eighteenth century; it is, at all events, so generally true now that considering it a token of social decadence is like crying out upon a wart as evidence of mortality.

It is a topheavy society we inhabit—one consequence of our having cultivated for so many years that self-destroying slogan, "equality of opportunity." What it means is clearly equal opportunity to achieve inequality; an achieved inequality in one generation clearly carries over into the next. How can one prevent a man who has achieved status and money from giving his children "the advantages?" Even if one could arrange things that way, is there any convincing reason to do so? Diminish a man's power to build something permanent for himself and his family, and you diminish his incentives to do anything at all. Children of achievers may have special abilities to achieve that way; why not cultivate them? What is disagreeable, in any case, is not what happens when Johann Sebastian Bach's offspring are blessed with musical talent but when the sons of the house of Johns Manville, with none of their parent's enterprise or ability, inherit his millions. Heavy inheritance taxes are not the answer; they have a way of making it impossible for a deserving son to carry on his father's farm. But the common attrition of lucky money does a good deal to lift the dead hand of inherited wealth. Wastrels and ne'er-do-wells—decadent scions of a once-great house—function like bacteria to get unearned money back into circulation. Generation after generation of skinflint Rockefellers, cut on the pattern of the original John D., would be a national affliction; it is good that we have had some lavish givers, and the health of American society would not suffer from a generation or two of Rockefeller dope addicts and Neronian voluptuaries. Not all private vices are public benefits, but some are; and in a society threatened with stagnation, they are probably those that stimulate, one way or another, the general circulation.

If anywhere, rotation in America needs energizing at top and bottom, by getting rid of entrenched fogies in the seats of power and developing the marketable skills of those at the foot of the economic ladder. Both actions call for a high order of social imagination. With an increased life span ahead of him, it is too boring for a man of energy to contemplate a quarter-century of golf, square dancing, and mental passivity.

Two or three careers may be needed to fill a full existence; the machinery for such mobility, starting with the very concept itself, is in need of radical development. Even grimmer is the prospect facing those just now starting their rise up the economic ladder. These are not necessarily the latest comers: Vietnamese, many Hispanics, and of course recent European immigrants seem generally able to take care of themselves. But the accumulation of embittered rejects in American slums—of different ethnic backgrounds, but contributing alike to a gang culture they have in common—represents a national problem that needs no emphasis. How are young men trained in the ghettos and barrios to a life of drugs, pimping, knives, and tire chains going to get into the American mainstream? The only answer is some sort of education. But where does one find, in a society that values above all the managerial position, the rank and status job, people to do the careful and painstaking, often dangerous, work of basic training in the "bad" schools? The society despises even grade teachers in "good" schools; it invests with a wholly artificial glamor the university professor, or better yet the university vice-president, whose immersion in paper shuffling frees him from mere teaching. Indeed, there are in some slum schools a few talented and dedicated teachers—just enough to suggest the possibilities, if a serious effort were made. But the values of the society are dead set against them. And by the time slum kids get into their teens, too many of them have set in a mold that will make future learning of any sort practically impossible.

Always there has been somebody at the bottom of America's economic ladder—you cannot have a ladder without a bottom rung. But that the same groups should remain for years and years at the bottom, hardening in their attitudes, festering in their despair, can only be an exceedingly ill symptom of a gangrenous member in an otherwise vital society. Though less grim to contemplate, it would be equally ominous if a narrow, inflexible group were able to monopolize for years on end positions at the top of the scale. Outsiders have to push their way in; some of the conditions that make it possible for them to do so are enervation, apathy, and mental stagnation on the part of the "old gang." They may not recognize these conditions as amounting to decadence, but the world will do them the favor.

In a word, elements of decomposition in a community may threaten its demise or reinforce its vitality as they maintain and enlarge or limit and destroy its capacity for creative change. There is nothing mechanical about this; the same threatening conditions that reduce some citizens to helpless distress animate others to heroic vigor.* Thus the decadence of a nation is not merely a social condition; it always has a large psychological component, which in a liberal and relativistic society is curiously hard to estimate.

For individuals in an individualistic society do not commonly spend more than a bare fraction of their time considering whether the society as a whole is healthy or decadent. The question doesn't grab them; they don't have the natural vocabulary for cosmic judgments of that sort. Their patriotism tends to be embarrassed and constrained, their very com-

---

*Montesquieu says (*Grandeur et décadence*) that civil war brings unusual vitality to the life of nations. Everyone becomes a soldier; great men come to the fore. This is one response to extreme challenge; comic contrast was provided recently by some young men who said mournfully to a television camera that if they couldn't get government loans, they would be forced to leave college forever. I doubt they meant it, but if they were sincere, they shouldn't have been going to college in the first place. Not one of them, while on camera, so much as contemplated the possibility of what used to be known, in more primitive times, as "working my way through college."

plaints about the scoundrels in power muted with comedy. But their speech is not and does not pretend to be a total expression of their feelings. Nobody in America talks about "building capitalism," as in other parts of the world they talk about "building socialism." The common rhetorical form is that we're just minding our own business, or doing our job, or getting along. That's what most people are doing, and as a by-product they make a society of a certain form, with a certain tone, with which nobody is completely happy, but which in crisis has a way of pulling itself together rather surprisingly. Ours is a slovenly, undisciplined society, addicted to taking the short view; when those vices come under challenge, it can sometimes assume some remarkably efficient and curiously general virtues. It would be a jejune destiny indeed to spend one's life, like the hero of Henry James's "The Beast in the Jungle," waiting for decadence to happen—only to have to settle for a rain check. The road of history has many junctions and bottlenecks, but no visible end. Peering down it, we see through the mists and uncertainties of contingent occasions three weird sisters: the violent and irregular importunities of technology, the blurry righteousness of bourgeois morality, the dead weight of petrified and powerfully organized opinion. Others could no doubt be added, but these will do. They are dangers, but not necessarily mortal—or if mortal, not on a fixed time scale. About the year 535 (shortly after the terrible insurrection against Justinian in Constantinople), when Byzantium had just celebrated its two-hundredth anniversary, its leaders might have stared into the future, and seen ogres, no fewer and no less fearful. But they hardened their minds to change, adapt, adjust, temporize, equivocate, compete, deceive, and if necessary fight—to navigate, in a word, the cruel seas in which fate had placed them. They were still doing it nine hundred and eighteen years later.

The Present Instance

With untypical modesty—as some will say—I have declined the question whether the human race as a whole isn't in some sort of decadence. There is nothing with which to make the comparison on which sensible use of the word depends. Still, if one looks at the world community, which is such a new and unprecedented thing in itself—surveying mankind from China to Peru—the difficulties of American society that lead popular propagandists to declare us decadent seem, though different in shape and degree, to be much the same in kind as those that afflict the rest of the human race. Multiplying numbers cry out for a fairer sharing of limited resources; racial hatreds and territorial jealousies tear at the fragile fabric of peace; wretched poverty jostles opulent wealth and unchallenged privilege; civilized communication is threatened by bestial rage. What makes these world conditions seem worse (most of them, in one form or another, have afflicted the human race since Adam or, at any rate, Noah) is that we know so much more about them. We feel, and actually are, closer to men ten thousand miles away than one medieval village was to another only thirty miles off. As the world shrinks, its brutalities and inequities become more glaring, and the consequences of having only a tragically incompetent central authority seem more terrible. It is an extremely bad scene. But Montaigne has a wry and relevant point of view. Where everything is falling, nothing falls. There is, in fact, no longer a horizon; it is easy to discard even the memory of it. We seem to be falling down at a terrific pace, but perhaps we are falling, from another perspective, up. One alternative is as likely as the other. And for sure we are all falling together, some of us faster or slower than others, with variations now and then, each of them looking more enormous as our perspective is more myopic. If it does nothing else for us, the concept of decadence forces us to lengthen perspective and see the dreadful word across a spectrum, which like all spectrums can be split. To the question, Is America a decadent society? there are at least three answers, and two of them are *Yes*. But in this context *Yes* itself is not an unequivocal word. At one extreme of the spectrum, local decadence is an inevitable stage in a thoroughly healthy process of rotation; by declining, rotten ups make room for the rise of ambitious downs. At the other extreme, in astral time our star will go cold and our species will be replaced or disappear amid complete cosmic indifference: we are already part of that process. On the intermediate scale, Western civilization may disintegrate either gradually or abruptly. If the former, we or some parts of us may hold together long enough to rival Byzantium and challenge the judgment of decadence even from beyond the grave. If the latter, we shall probably be so absorbed in the specifics of the catastrophe that we will hardly recognize its total shape. As between the last two alternatives, the choice is to a considerable extent still in our own power, and nobody should pretend to judge impartially of his own event. We may be on the verge of total collapse tomorrow, but it behooves us to live as if we were sure of another thousand years.

Design by David Bullen
Typeset in Mergenthaler Cloister
by Wilsted and Taylor
Printed by Maple-Vail
on acid-free paper